3 1994 01301 6511

SANTA ANA PUBLIC LIBRARY

D0623847

SUCCULENTS
for the contemporary garden

Yvonne Cave

635.9525 CAV
Cave, Yvonne
Succulents for the
  contemporary garden

                        $29.95
CENTRAL   31994013016511

Timber Press

Acknowledgements

Since my first book on succulents, *The Succulent Garden*, interest in these special plants has increased markedly, and the range of genera and species available has extended, as has my own collection and experience in growing them.

I'm grateful to friends Clive and Nicki Higgie of Paloma Gardens, Wanganui, who allowed me to photograph in their exciting garden. Clive was patient with my many questions on propagation and lent me books from his extensive collection for detail checking.

Phyllis Williamson's echeveria collection inspired me to take more photographs and her help with the names of many cultivars is appreciated.

Photographs from the gardens or collections of Marlie Bell, Val Bieleski, Judy Foster, Bernice Jones, Joan Pollock, Mike Capenerhurst, New Plymouth Branch New Zealand Cactus and Succulent Club, Peak Perennials, Coromandel Cacti and Manurewa Botanic Garden broadened the range of plants depicted. Visits to Huntington Gardens in Los Angeles and to Japan widened the scope further.

Don Stephenson of Bason Botanic Gardens, Wanganui, kindly helped with name checking, an important aspect for this type of publication, and one that demands patience with the ever-changing botanical names.

Finally I must thank Jane Connor of Godwit/Random House/Timber Press for her enthusiasm over my photographs for this book, which I hope fills a gap in the horticultural field. Also my grateful thanks to Tom Beran of Random House for his work in seeing the project to publication, and Sarah Elworthy for her competence with the layout and design.

First published in North America and the United Kingdom in 2003 by
Timber Press, Inc.
The Haseltine Building
133 S.W. Second Avenue, Suite 450
Portland, Oregon 97204, USA
tel 1-800-327-5680 or 1-503-227-2878
fax 1-503-227-3070
www.timberpress.com

Reprinted 2005

© 2002 Yvonne Cave (text and photographs)

The moral rights of the author have been asserted

ISBN 0-88192-573-X

A CIP record for this book is available from the Library of Congress

Front cover photograph: *Kalanchoe* 'Bronze Sculpture'; back cover photographs (top to bottom): *Echeveria* 'After Glow' flowers; *Sempervivum* 'Director Jacobs'; *Yucca rigida*; *Argyroderma pearsonii*.

Book design and production: Sarah Elworthy

Printed in China

CONTENTS

INTRODUCTION

What are succulents and how do we define them?

Succulents or xerophytes are plants that nature has endowed with the ability to store water in reserve when it is available in good seasons, in case the next ones are extremely harsh and dry, and they have adapted some amazing shapes and forms in their struggle to survive. Some form a large water-storing base called a caudex, the shapes quite bizarre in some cases. Others have reduced surface area of their stems and leaves to cut back evaporation in extreme heat. Sometimes the leaves are modified to avoid the hot sun: any moisture collected in times of rain is stored within a shiny, waxy, felted or barked surface to avoid transpiration. Some plants have a very clever modification whereby they open their stomata or pores to breathe only in the cool of the night, which avoids moisture loss in the hottest part of the day. This feature is called Crassulacean Acidic Metabolism, and the plants in this group — aeoniums, cotyledon, echeverias and sempervivums — are known as CAM plants.

The great variety of form and subtle foliage colour makes these plants extremely attractive and useful for the gardener with dry areas to cope with. Dry sunny areas can range from hillsides, rockeries, rain-shadowed areas, sheltered borders against sunny walls, verandahs on high-rise buildings, patios and porches, to window ledges and, of course, containers.

Most succulents can stand windy sites, whether near the sea or on a rooftop garden, and will also tolerate a greater degree of neglect than any other plants. They do show their appreciation of a little tender loving care by growing stronger and with better texture, form and colour, although over-watering and feeding is detrimental and should be avoided. Simply by being observant, succulent growers will soon get to know when plants are in optimum health, neither starved nor overfed.

Dry areas aren't always sunny and some succulents cope well with semi-shade, some like gasterias and haworthias actually prefer it. Many of these succulents can be used to create form and interest to those special intimate areas of the garden or patio.

Even in housed succulent collections, successful growers find that some species need brighter spots in the enclosure while others are happier where light and heat from the sun are not so direct.

As with growing any plant, knowledge of the specific needs of that plant as well as your situation, climate and limitations are all important. Where I live on the sandy south-west coast of the North Island of New Zealand, I can grow many plants outdoors (not only succulents) that would be impossible inland only 50 km away unless under complete cover. The annual rainfall where I live ranges from 800–1200 mm, and the winter months are usually the wettest with occasional heavy falls in summer. Because New Zealand is a small dot in the large ocean, we suffer winds from all directions, but fortunately succulents seldom suffer from wind and it actually helps dry off moisture from the leaves that don't like being wet for long periods when the weather is cold. Even within one New Zealand garden there are little microclimates that allow certain plants to thrive, and this applies worldwide. For the new gardener, trial and error, or expert advice are the options, the latter being worthwhile when expensive plants are used.

Are there really connoisseurs of simple plants like succulents?

The answer is yes, there are many connoisseurs of succulents. Succulents are now extremely popular and there are so many available that selection is necessary. Their attributes need to be considered and the best-suited

---

Opposite, top: *Agave attenuata*, *Beaucarnea recurvata* and *Yucca gloriosa* give great textural quality to the garden.

Bottom: A newly planted rockery already giving colour and much promise after only two months, the senecios, echeverias and aeoniums all looking well settled for the summer.

---

species chosen, taking into account location and climate, and other requirements including style of growth, light factors and moisture.

Our connoisseur has probably had experience in growing these plants, developed an interest in certain types of succulents and can discriminate between species. Careful selection for artistic value, the aesthetic appearance, that aristocratic style apart from the strength and health of the plant all help to create final satisfaction for the avid collector or gardener.

The connoisseur uses their judgement to determine the choice of plants, reviews them from time to time and assesses their value within the collection or garden. Sometimes judicious pruning or even elimination of some species might be undertaken to observe quality and quantity, and this critical decision-making can take determination.

It is sometimes fashionable to own and cultivate plants known to be one of the rarest species available or to cost the earth, and fashion can also create connoisseurs.

All succulent enthusiasts enjoy these plants, whatever angle they are coming from. Because succulents are easy care, there is not the same worry of watering in hot weather, which can become a boring routine with plants that don't have the ability to store moisture. For busy

working families and the elderly, succulents can fulfil the need for tidy and colourful plants in many different areas around the home.

Succulents really are fun to work with. Because most of them can be increased quite quickly, the enthusiastic connoisseur can soon have very creative layouts or arrangements. There is so much diversity of form, colour and texture, more than in most other plants, for really imaginative landscaping, whether on a large or small scale.

And isn't it exciting to come home with a new and different succulent, either a special purchase or a generous friend's shared treasure.

Mention should be made of cacti, which are also succulents, but are not dealt with in this book. True cacti produce little clusters of white hairs called areoles on the edges or body of the plant and it is from these that groups of prickles arise. Agaves and others have spines and teeth, but they are produced singly, not in clusters. The succulents in this book generally belong to the 'user friendly' group, although you might wonder when you get too close to an agave!

Container-grown plants need occasional re-potting after 2–3 years, but the satisfaction of the revitalised planting is worth the small effort involved. Outdoor groups of succulents are also better for a makeover after several years, although some maintain a good appearance for 5–8 years, but when one considers the number of years with very little maintenance compared with other plants, the value of a succulent planting is high.

By now you will have noticed that I am a succulent connoisseur and am happy to admit it. After about 50 years of growing succulents in my garden, I cannot imagine gardening without them. If I have to move to a smaller place one day there would always be a porch, an area under the eaves or a space for containers that would be taken up with some of my favourites. The selection I currently grow for their colour and form give me great pleasure in several areas of the garden, in groups of different species that either complement or contrast in some way. When I lay out groups of succulents in new areas I feel that I am 'painting the gardenscape', a very satisfying exercise. Although succulent plants are brittle to handle they're very obliging and don't complain about being moved around at any time.

In contrast to my style of planting, many landscapers have created successful plantings of succulents in a minimalist style, with just a few sculptural plants set in areas of gravel or raked stones. These are also very easy to maintain and suitable for certain areas but can lack colour, something that seems a pity as they can have such subtle tones.

When my aunt gave me some succulents in the early 1950s, they were called 'jelly beans' and 'hen and chickens', and those were the only names I had heard of for these plants. My aunt advised me that the 'red one' would grow from leaves and the 'round ones' would grow babies around the sides. They did and later she gave me a 'blue one' and a 'green one' and they did too! Eventually I was able to cover the hot sandy soil around some small conifers with very colourful groups of these succulents and it was a most successful planting for many years while I was busy with a young family.

Gradually I found a few new species to try despite succulents being nonexistent in nurseries and hard to find, kind friends sometimes shared plants that had long been neglected in their gardens.

It wasn't until 1995 that I had to look very seriously at naming my succulents. With many photographs of these plants on hand and a proposition for a book about succulents to prepare, the hunt was on to find names. Most gardeners were as ignorant as I was about names for succulents, probably because any they grew had been handed on without names. Very few publications at that time featured photographs of succulents that were useful for identification although cacti had quite a share of the market. However, I found enough names for captions on my photographs in the book *The Succulent Garden*, which has introduced many people to the pleasure of succulents.

Since then, several warm dry summers with water rationing and threats of global warming have made many gardeners aware that xerophytic plants are very worthwhile. Demand has increased accordingly for succulents and nurseries and garden centres are now more conscious of these plants, and have learnt that shade and constant watering are not necessary and are in fact

damaging to many succulents.

Now that we have reached the connoisseur stage with our succulents, the range of extra genera and species covered in this publication will hopefully be appreciated. Many cultivars in genera such as Echeveria are very hard to positively identify by name as they are so much alike, and might even be known by another name in a different place or country. According to historical references from botanists, nomenclature has been difficult for several hundred years, since the days of the very early explorers, and there are still changes coming through all the time.

For the purposes of this book, every endeavour has been made to use names currently recommended by the Royal Horticultural Society or Index Kewensis and other recognised Botanic Gardens and growers.

Above: An amazing accent of blue with *Senecio mandraliscae*, enhanced by the contrast of *Echeveria gibbiflora* and *Aeonium decorum*.

Opposite: *Aloe plicatilis*, *Agave americana*, beaucarnea, furcraea and other plants with interesting textural qualities.

CULTIVATION
Outdoors

When growing plants that store moisture, like succulents, it is important to remember that they live naturally in dry to arid parts of the world so don't need to be kept permanently wet. In areas of frequent rainfall there are ways to help keep the roots from becoming waterlogged: very porous soil mixes, planting on sloping grounds that face the sun to aid drainage, and the use of partial coverings during the wettest season. When planting agaves for instance, instead of digging a deep hole in heavy ground that might fill with water, make a wide shallow hole with a slightly mounded central area that the basal crown can rest over while the roots spread out.

We should all look at the many dry areas against buildings and walls which shield the prevailing rain from the ground, but are very warm and sunny and often very difficult for gardening, as these are the ideal spots for succulents. Whether plantings consist of the large-growing succulents such as furcraeas, dracaenas or euphorbias, or the smaller echeverias, sedums and aeoniums depends entirely on the space available, the amount of care available and the requirement of colour. Succulents last longer and require less maintenance than many annuals and perennials, and very attractive groupings can be so easily laid out.

Gravel or stones are a very effective medium for covering the ground around succulents, but an alternative to these is using massed groups of smaller succulents such as the blue senecios and red, green or blue-grey sedums to bring colour into the planting area, and the combination of taller plants and groundcovering types works very well.

Warm spring or autumn are usually the best planting seasons for succulents, and certainly *not* in the cold of winter.

Many succulents will need replanting over time, but this depends on the plants grown and the climatic conditions of that part of the world. A number of groupings I have worked with have needed little maintenance and been very satisfactory for 5 years or more, apart from occasional weeding (before the weeds disperse new seeds).

A replant is easy with many of the smaller types like aeoniums, echeverias and sedums. The simplest solution is to cut off a number of good crowns, each with a short stem, and leave to dry on trays in the shade for one or more days. In the meantime remove the remaining plants and lightly cultivate the soil. Mix in a little slow-release fertiliser and replant the pieces, perhaps in a different layout this time to enhance the colour balance or shape of the group. Replanting is best done during early autumn when the ground is still warm and if very dry, water lightly at first and then again after about a week — growth will soon take place.

Newly prepared and replanted ground usually grows weeds quite quickly and these need to be dealt with, by hand if in a dense planting, taking care not to break the brittle succulents. A second weed crop usually appears later and again hand weeding is essential to eliminate weeds before they seed. This all sounds very tedious but the good news is that from then on the succulents will fill over the ground well, and providing the soil is not disturbed or cultivated too much during weeding, less weeds will germinate.

When the ground under succulents is covered with gravel or stones an occasional spray with a herbicide, such as Roundup to control small weed seedlings can be used, taking care that the succulents aren't splashed. Organic alternatives are hand weeding and the use of small flame or steam sprayers.

Further maintenance of this type of succulent really only involves cutting off the deadheads after flowering and sometimes spraying for aphids which can attack the buds or new shoots on some species.

Larger-growing succulents also need an occasional tidy up by removing older lower leaves and spent flowerheads to maintain and show off their special shape and form.

It is also important to keep all succulents clear of leaf litter from other trees and plants, particularly in wet conditions when the rubbish can cause rotting.

I have mentioned wet ground and its drainage being crucial to successful growing, but other places with poor dry sandy soils can also be successfully planted with some assistance. The addition of a little good topsoil or very well-decayed composted materials plus some slow-release

fertiliser will create a suitable area for planting. I had a rockery of poor sand that had not been cleared of many old shrubs and creepers for about 40 years in my garden, and I worked partly composted sawdust mulch from a calf shed into the pockets of the sand and added a slow-release fertiliser, and in 6 months the growth of my succulents was remarkable. The sawdust mulch doesn't have much food value, but helps to break up and aerate the fine iron sand of the area which repels water when very dry. However, any commercially available coarse soil mixes with slow-release fertiliser included would have had the same effect.

Cold winter conditions with persistent rain and occasional frosts can cause leaf rotting on many of the soft smaller-growing succulents like echeverias. Through trial and error I have made temporary covers that keep the wet and frost off some groups of succulents for about two and a half months, so that the plants will look well when visitors arrive in early spring. Plastic conduit piping is useful for bending into hoops, and with plastic sheeting stretched over the top and taped to the piping, this winter shelter offers great protection over quite a large area.

The plants are kept dry and really flourish in their winter house, which I've found doesn't need to be right to the ground, enabling the plants to be seen rather than lost from view. I have also made smaller shelters for 6–8 medium-sized echeverias from 2 sections of wirenetting 1 m long by 70 cm wide, which are bent lengthwise to form a tunnel shape, and a sheet of similar-sized plastic placed between them.

Succulents can withstand quite heavy frosts and cold if they're kept dry, both overhead and in the ground. As I write this, a frost of -4 to -5°C has touched up some of my uncovered succulents, but almost all those under the plastic covers are fine. In general, aeoniums and kalanchoes seem to be affected by frost more than most other genera.

Seasonal changes that allow plants to take up more moisture than usual and become flaccid limit their ability to withstand frost. Dry conditions harden succulents to weather fluctuations of temperature, leaving them less likely to suffer as badly in moderate frosts.

Container growing

Succulents really are fun to grow in containers because they don't complain or suffer when neglected like most other pot plants do. Instead of constantly replacing very tired or spent plants, containers of succulents that have been selected for growth style and colour groupings can be successfully grown for up to three years, some even

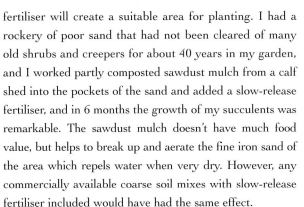

Above left: Plastic piping bent into hoops makes an excellent winter shelter for a large area of succulents; above right: A smaller shelter is created using wirenetting and plastic.

longer, before repotting is necessary.

A free-draining potting mix with added slow-release fertiliser is necessary, and containers must have at least one good drainage hole. The frequency of watering is a difficult one, as locations vary so much, and the size and number of plants, the size of the container, the water-retaining propensity of the mix used and the time of year and temperature must all be taken into account. The safest way to check moisture content is to dig down about 6 cm with a sharp trowel or knife. Once completely dry, some mixes need soaking to make them retain moisture again, as watering from the top won't always hold — the water just runs straight through and out the bottom. To make sure that some water is retained, stand the container in deep water until moisture shows all over the top surface and then allow to drain freely. A good soaking like this occasionally is much better than trying to wet the top surface and never knowing if the roots have seen any moisture at all.

Experience soon tells whether the plants look well, but signs of wrinkling or shrinking in summer indicate extreme dryness, however, over-watering can cause roots to rot and the plant to collapse. Sometimes the first signs of over-watering are many leaves dropping off or patches of rot appearing. Where I live, most succulents grow better if watered well about once every ten days in hot weather and full sun, but during the winter they are best left dry for weeks on end, even months for succulents like lithops which have normal winter wrinkling (others are indicated in their specific entries).

Mildew in dry late summer conditions is sometimes seen on echeverias, usually the big frilly ones, and can disfigure their large leaves. Fungicide helps to control this, although the spray can leave a whitish residue in the leaf hollows.

Container-grown plants held in dry sheltered places are more likely to fall victim to mealy bugs and aphids than those in the ground, but these can be controlled with insecticides. Sometimes it is suggested that mealy bugs are swabbed with methylated spirits on a cotton bud, but there are usually numerous minute juvenile bugs invisible to the naked eye, so a spray that covers all is more likely to provide successful treatment and control.

Container-grown succulents for shady areas

When growing succulents in containers either outdoors or in semi-covered areas, it is possible to place and plant

Below: *Agave franzosinii, Aeonium arboreum* 'Schwartzkopf' and *Crassula coccinea* thrive in a hot corner.

containers according to their requirements of full sunlight or partial sun and shade. Most succulents like plenty of sunlight, but if you want to plant up a container for a shady but dry spot, look through the listings of *Aeonium tabulaeform, Cotyledon tomentosa* ssp. *ladismithiensis*, gasterias, some kalanchoes, haworthias and sempervivums for plants that will be successful. *Agave attenuata, Yucca elephantipes* and *Yucca gloriosa* can also tolerate a certain amount of shade and will make a bold statement.

Indoor housed collections

Many of the more serious succulent collectors have completely housed collections, and when these are well managed they are most impressive. Even in unheated glasshouses the temperature is usually more even than outdoors, and most plants do better if the fluctuations aren't too great. It is always very hard to maintain an even temperature in a covered house as some areas can overheat while other pockets are too cold. Ventilation techniques can help overcome some of these problems (often at a great expense, however), for the serious or professional grower, but for the average home enthusiast there is a certain amount of trial and error. Management of a house will also vary considerably from country to country according to the very different climatic conditions around the world.

The types of succulents grown demand different treatments. A monoculture would be easier to manage in a house than a hundred different succulents, but if there are successful growers in your area they will know your climatic conditions well, so discuss management strategies with them and learn from their experiences.

Watering plants indoors is often better done manually rather than automatically, especially when a range of different succulents are grown as some species or cultivars will require more than others. Regular monitoring is still important with manual watering.

As with any container growing there can be problems with mildew and aphids, but spider mites are an added problem in housed collections as they enjoy the enclosed conditions, browsing on the plants' surfaces causing browning.

PESTS & DISEASES

Fortunately succulents don't suffer from many pests and diseases, and the few that are problematic can be dealt with fairly easily. One of the most important factors is to be observant and notice a problem before it becomes a major one on your plants.

The use of biological control agents or predatory insects to attack the bad ones on our plants is increasing. There are now stockists of agents to control aphids, spider mites, thrips and mealy bugs, mainly for use in greenhouses where air temperatures can be controlled, but this is a major step in assisting specialist growers.

Slugs and snails

Slugs and snails eat holes in succulents as they do in other plants, some preferring the edges of leaves. At the first sign of chewing, clear away all the hiding places in old litter from around and near the plants, and use slug and snail pellets according to the instructions on the packet.

Flying beetles

Occasionally night-flying grass grub beetles fly on to the top of plants, bite scattered holes for a few nights and then disappear. Aeoniums and echeverias seem to be particularly susceptible. If any damage is seen spray immediately with an insecticide, using a spreader to help it stick on the smooth leaves.

Mealy bugs

These occur in container-grown and indoor collections, usually under leaves and stems in dark sheltered dry spots. Mealy bugs have small white fluffy bodies and produce many young. Spray with insecticide using a spreader to ensure it reaches all areas, and repeat after a week or 10 days. Alternatively, the whole plant, pot and mix can be soaked in a bucket or can of spray for 5 minutes, or until the mix is thoroughly wetted. When the infestation is bad, mealy bugs will go down into the mix and feed on the roots, so soaking usually rids the plant of those ones too.

An old-fashioned method is to touch the mealy bugs with a cotton bud dipped in methylated spirits, but this doesn't eliminate all the minute ones that you can't see.

Aphids

These often move to the flower buds of succulents and occasionally on soft new growth. An insecticide used as per the instructions is the best way to deal with them quickly; soapy water sprayed on them every few days will check them, but not as fast or finally as insecticide.

Spider mites

Spider mites are minute and create nasty brown patches on the skin of indoor grown succulents, usually starting from the basal area. It is difficult to spray insecticide on plants with tightly clustered leaves, but dipping the whole plant, roots and mix into a container of insecticide for a few minutes seems very effective. The damaged skin areas don't recover, so early detection of the problem is important in saving your plant from their disfiguring efforts.

Scale

I've only seen scale once on succulents and they were small dark brown ones. Scale insects live under a hard shell firmly attached to the stem or leaf and are hard to get rid of. An insecticide with the addition of spraying oil is recommended for all scale insects, but oil doesn't look good on succulents that have a bloom on the leaves. However, it is worth using to eliminate the scale before they spread to other plants.

Black spot in winter

During cold wet weather, a round black spot disfigures some of my echeverias, particularly *Echeveria gibbiflora*, but I've found that picking up all the old leaves from under the plants in late autumn and spraying the plants and ground under them with fungicide has helped this problem.

Mildew

Mildew is often hard to see in the early stages because of the bloom on plants such as echeverias, but early detection and treatment can stop it spreading. Most of the powder-based fungicides leave a residue on the leaves, although that is preferable to the scarring mildew causes, but liquid based sprays hardly mark the foliage. Organic alternatives such as milk, oil and bicarbonate of soda would all leave residue, some of it powdery, and the milk and oil will mark the bloom on the leaves.

PROPAGATION

Propagation is easy with most succulents — some even get on with it themselves — although often the slowest or most difficult ones are the special species or cultivars we want more of. The easiest succulents are those that send out new plants from their base, the new crowns soon forming their own roots, or those that layer, rooting where they touch the ground. Others grow from leaves dropped on the ground and some root easily from cuttings.

Offsets and suckers

Some succulents, including a number of the echeverias send out new plants or offsets from the base, *Echeveria elgans* and *E. secunda* being examples. Sempervivums do the same, and some have quite long 'apron strings' as they settle down to grow their own roots. Aloes and agaves are usually easily propagated, aloes from basal crowns that appear around the plant stem which can be cut off cleanly, sometimes all ready to grow with a few roots. Agaves form offsets or suckers that sometimes arise a distance from the parent crown. In this case, the stem that has come from the parent is cut cleanly and the new rooted plant dug out. Plant into a container of coarse mix or straight into free-draining ground in warm weather.

Below: Excellent use of succulents for contrasts of shape and colour.

Bulbils and plantlets

Furcraeas produce many fully formed bulbils on their enormous flowerheads, these have a heavy base, a few leaves and sometimes even a small root, and will drop to the ground ready to grow. Plantlets are produced by some of the kalanchoes as tiny formed plants on the edges of the parent's leaves. These drop off freely and can even be a nuisance when too prolific. They will grow upright on free-draining ground or set on the top of pots of coarse mix.

Divisions

Divisions have to be forcibly made on plants that have tight multiple crowns such as dyckias. In this case a sharp-pointed spade is necessary to cut sections from the plant, making sure there is a fully formed crown with roots. In the smaller plant range, *Crassula* 'Morgan's Beauty' grows in a tight cluster and can have pieces with a firm stem cut out and re-rooted.

Most divisions root easily in a coarse medium such as pumice when kept fairly warm and dry.

Stem cuttings

Cuttings from succulents usually grow naturally and better in warm weather conditions of 20–30°C, but bottom heat can be used, and the rules of dusting the cut stem with flowers of sulphur and leaving to dry before planting are important. Soft succulent stems tend to rot, so leave at least 24 hours after cutting before planting in a slightly damp coarse potting medium, like sand or pumice. If the temperature at the time is cool, a longer drying period could be given. Because there is no great hurry to plant cuttings of succulents, this gives great flexibility of timing when replanting areas of massed small-growing succulents. A number of cuttings can be cut from the old plants and set aside for a week or more in a shady spot ready to plant when the ground has been prepared for replanting. In the case of bedding plants I don't bother to dust with sulphur but dry them well and plant into barely damp sandy soil with slow-release fertiliser previously worked in.

A light watering after planting dried cuttings into the ground and again a few days later should get them underway, particularly if planted while the weather is warm. Among those easy to grow from stem cuttings are cotyledons, aeoniums and kalanchoes. Top-heavy cuttings are hard to keep upright, but there is no great advantage in having a long stem — keep it in balance with the top; the number of leaves can also be reduced. A small stake and tie are advantageous in some situations.

When cuttings of special succulents are pot grown, you can gently feel that the stem is firm in the potting mix and once you are sure that it has rooted, pot it on into a regular free-draining mix.

Echeverias that have become leggy can be rejuvenated by cutting the stem off about 5 cm below the leaves, dusting the cut with flowers of sulphur and suspending the crown over a small pot in a warm light area. Roots will form on the stem in a few weeks and the rejuvenated plant can then be replanted in a slightly damp potting mix. The flower stems of a few of the big echeverias will sometimes grow plantlets from the leaf nodules after being stood in pots of mix or laid on trays of soil mix in the shade. They take a long while, sometimes months, to form these little plantlets that can be carefully removed and potted on as exact replicas of the parent. Those that have already formed roots grow on much quicker than those without.

Aerial roots

These sometimes form under branches of some aeoniums and other succulents, making propagation very easy. Cut the branch or the crown from the plant above the root zone and place in free-draining ground or mix.

Leaf cuttings

Not all succulents will grow from leaves, but some genera develop baby plants and roots from mature leaves left on the ground or potting mix. Some echeverias, gasterias, graptopetalum, kalanchoe and sedums grow freely while others will not. Trial and error are necessary, but with all leaf cuttings, the leaf must come away cleanly from the stem with an almost sealed end. If they are broken off, look wet and show the flesh inside the leaf, they will not grow.

Kalanchoe beharense can be grown from sections of the leaf stem and *K. tomentosa* leaves left on top of the mix will form new leaves and roots. Warm conditions are necessary.

Seed

Many succulents can be grown from seed, this being the only way to bring certain species to a country where restrictions prohibit the entry of live plants, although seed is also scrutinised. Because some succulents don't produce offsets, can't be divided and don't have cutting material available, seed is often the only way of propagation.

Aloe ferox and *A. polyphlla* seldom have offsets, nor do some of the agaves and yuccas. In the small plant range, lithops and some of the other thick-leafed genera are best raised from seed as dividing them can lead to rotting.

The seed of many succulents is very fine and best sown in warm temperatures of 20–30°C. Sprinkle evenly over the surface of a sterilised seed-raising mix or coarse river sand that has been thoroughly moistened, perhaps by standing in a container of water the day before. Fine seeds don't need covering, and the larger ones only need covering to the depth of the seeds.

Lightly moisten with a fine mister and cover the tray or pot with plastic film supported by a wire hoop. Mist again a day later and place a little water in a shallow container under the pot for capillary action watering. Place away from direct sunshine.

Germination can take from 3 days to 3 weeks, so check every few days. Some stapelias can take just 3 days, but aloes and agaves might need a full 21 days. The freshness of the seed and temperature and moisture levels are all factors in germination. If any damping off appears, mist with a fungicide during the warmth of the day.

Once germination is complete, gradually open up the covering about 3 cm more each day to let in more light and reduce the humidity. This is all much easier to control if under the cover of a glasshouse or porch. Keep moisture in the saucer underneath, and if necessary a quarter-strength liquid fertiliser could occasionally be used.

When seedlings are big enough to handle, about 5 mm, they can be pricked out, taking care not to damage their delicate roots or crush the leaves. Some could be large enough in 5–6 weeks while others might take 2 years as there is a great variation in the different genera.

Move the seedlings into a mix that contains any combination of sand, gravel, pumice, bark and a little humus with the addition of a slow-release fertiliser. Some of the commercial mixes are suitable while some people prefer to make their own, but the crucial factor is the free-draining capacity of the mix. Keep the seedlings in good even light and do not overwater.

Tiny seedlings are hard to lift out of a pot, so try gently sliding the whole lot out onto a bench where they can be safely lifted out of the mix without damage. When the roots are long, make a hole in the new pot of mix with a dibber so that the long roots can be dropped in freely and the mix gently pushed around the leaves, keeping them at the same level as they were in the seed-raising mix. A little dry sand sprinkled on the surface keeps the lower leaves from getting too wet.

Repot when necessary. This will depend on the genera as some are slow growers and others fast and large, and gradually harden off the plants to full outdoors light if they're to go in outdoor containers or planted outside.

ADENIA

Passifloraceae

Adenias come from East Africa, Transvaal in South Africa, Namibia, Somalia, Botswana and the Middle East. They are noted for the huge caudex that can be up to 1 m tall and 2 m in diameter. Some species are spiny, and all produce thin stems on numerous, somewhat tangled branches; tendrils appear on the leafy stems of *Adenia digitata*. All species have yellow or yellow-green flowers with small leaves.

Adenia glauca

From arid tropical areas of East Africa, this weird plant with a massive caudex sends up slender branches during the growing season. Some species have bases to about 1 m across. An indoor plant, unless the climate is similar to its homeland. Propagation from seed.

ADENIUM

Apocynaceae

Adeniums are caudiciforms, their caudexes forming either above or below ground and grow to 2 m tall. They have glossy green leaves and thick succulent stems. Flowers are funnel-shaped, last 2–5 days and vary from pink to red. Cultivar 'Asha' has pink flowers 12 cm in diameter, while the species are about 5 cm. Temperatures above 26°C, water and a rich soil with full sun are needed, as these plants are deciduous in air temperatures below 10°C. Over-watering causes basal rot; water less in their dormant season.

Adenium obesum 'The Desert Rose'

From East Africa and the Middle East, this forms a spreading bush up to 2 m, with a thick twisted fleshy base with short branches and glossy dark green leaves about 8 cm long. Clusters of 5 cm flowers range from red to pink, purple and white. Propagation from seed shows variable forms.

Above: *Adenia glauca*.

Right: *Adenium obesum* 'The Desert Rose'.

AEONIUM

Crassulaceae

There are many different species of aeoniums, most of which come from the warm Canary Islands, Cape Verde Isles and Morocco. More species are becoming available as interest in succulents increases. They are excellent garden plants ranging through a variety of forms from branching plants up to 1.5 m in height to groundcovers; some are also suitable for container growing. Aeoniums can tolerate dry conditions, although some species tend to drop leaves in the heat of summer. They are very closely related to sempervivums, although aeoniums are not as tolerant of heavy frosts as their hardier relations. Propagation of the tall growers can be from stem cuttings with a cluster of leaves on the top, the cut stem dried before planting. Semi-rooted pieces can be taken from near the base of some species, while *Aeonium decorum tricolor* and some others produce aerial roots from the lower branches. Once cut off and planted they grow freely. The leaves of

A. *tabulaeform* will form small plantlets from the stem end if inserted in a dryish medium such as pumice.

Aeonium arboreum var. arboreum (syn. A. manriqueorum)

This has a very dramatic large rosette of green leaves, with a hint of a narrow red edge; the leaves are held upright around the recessed central area of growth.

Aeonium atropurpureum

With its attractive summer bronzing and green centres, this looks great in clumps which grow to about 1.5 m high. Pruning to keep the plants compact is very worthwhile.

Aeonium atropurpureum 'Schwartzkopf'

This is the very dark form of A. *atropurpureum*, which can also reach 1.5 m, providing wonderful colour and contrast in the garden. When plants of any of the tall aeoniums get to 1 m it is advisable to prune some of the larger heads out before the weight at the top proves too much for the root system to hold up. The brilliant yellow cones of small starry flowers that appear in late winter are very showy, but the plant won't flower until the crowns are quite large and the stems thick, which could take 2–3 years from planting. In areas with high summer heat and humidity these plants can suffer a heavy leaf drop for a time, but they soon recover. Full light is necessary for this species to colour well and should the shade of a growing tree reach the plant it will gradually change from dark maroon to green.

Aeonium decorum 'Sunburst'

A variegated cultivar seen at Huntington Gardens, Los Angeles. It differs from *A. decorum tricolor* in that the leaves are narrower, flatter and less incurved. The red edge is narrowly defined and the cream colouring is lighter than the other cultivar.

Aeonium decorum tricolor

This branching plant with bright red-edged leaves variegated with yellow, makes a very colourful low bush that grows to about 35 cm high. The small cream flowers in a raceme above the foliage are quite attractive, but each flowering branch is better pruned off as they don't seem to grow well after flowering. *A. decorum tricolor* doesn't appreciate

This page, top: *Aeonium atropurpureum* 'Schwartzkopf'; right: *A. decorum tricolor*; below: *A. decorum* 'Sunburst'.

Opposite, left: *Aeonium arboreum* var. *arboreum*; right: *A. atropurpureum*.

frost. Aerial roots are put down by some of the branches, making propagation very easy.

Aeonium 'Frosty'

With its silvery leaves, sometimes with a flush of red on the ends, this is a fast-growing and useful groundcovering plant. Yellow flowers are held above the foliage.

Aeonium spectabilis

A small branching aeonium that grows to about 30 cm. It has small leaves up to 2 cm long, which are green with a reddish tinge when the plant is dry.

Aeonium subplanum

This has a large flattish rosette of deep green leaves, which look bold planted near finer-leaved plants. Numerous plantlets are formed on the stem, so propagation is easy.

Aeonium tabulaeform

This species from the Canary Islands is notable for its wide flat-topped rosettes of numerous green leaves edged with silver hairs. It will eventually put up an inflorescence of yellow flowers from the centre of the flat disc. In its native habitat A. tabulaeform is said to grow on banks with the flat top held on an angle so that water is shed very quickly from the leaves. This plant enjoys semi-shade. Older leaves taken from under the disc can be used to propagate young plants, but sometimes offsets are formed from the main stem of the plant and are easy to take off and grow on.

This page, top: Aeonium 'Frosty'; bottom: A. subplanum.

Opposite, top: Aeonium undulatum pseudo tabulaeform; bottom left: A. undulatum; bottom right: A. tabulaeform.

Aeonium undulatum

This has very large rosettes, 15–30 cm in diameter, of rounded green leaves with a fine red edge on the outer margins. Stout stems can reach about 1.5 m, and the inflorescence of small yellow flowers, growing up to 40 cm by 25 cm, rises from a crown.

Aeonium undulatum pseudo tabulaeform

This is a bunching plant that produces many crowns of green leaves in a tidy manner, very useful for a container or the garden.

AGAVE

Agavaceae

There are over 300 named agaves ranging from the smaller species at 30 cm to giants of 6 m in diameter. Sword-like leaves and perfectly symmetrical formations are typical of these plants, which are native to Mexico, tropical America and the West Indies.

Foliage colours vary from deep green to silvery blue with the teeth (there are some exceptions) on the leaf margins either blending or contrasting. The variegated forms make handsome specimen plants. Almost all agaves have a very hard sharp terminal spine on each leaf, so when plants are near the edge of a walking area it is advisable to prune these off for safety. A mature plant with teeth and terminal spines standing out is a fearsome thing — they're not plants for the very small garden or the timid grower.

Fortunately there are a few agaves without spines of any sort, and one of the best for more intimate areas of the garden is *Agave attenuata*. Its broad glaucus leaves make a bold statement in the garden.

Agaves are magnificent, whether showing the wonderful embossed patterns left as imprints on the unfurling tight leaf bud or dominating the landscape with a flowering candelabra 4 m high. Flowering agaves are spectacular, some being amazingly tall, and the yellow flowers produced by a number of them stand out against a blue sky; honey-eating birds appreciate the flowers and can be seen flying from one species to another in large gardens.

Long before synthetic fibres were introduced *A. sisalana* was grown for its tough sisal hemp fibres, even today many species are still grown for fibre.

Several by-products are extracted from the agave fibre operations in Mexico and East Africa, one of them a sapogenin which is used in the manufacture of steroids. In surveys done during the 1950s it was found that *A. vilmoriniana* produced higher levels of sapogenin than the agaves more commonly grown for fibre, and was not only their equal in fibre production but reproduced vegetatively and required a similar amount of ground space. Whether or not this resource has been developed is unclear.

Research has been undertaken into the nutritional qualities of agave leaves — the juice is rich in sugar, and when treated can be made into refreshing drinks; the squeezed leaves can then be turned into ensilage for stock food. Perhaps further work on the use of these secondary by-products of the agave should be undertaken, especially in the poorer third world countries that have the climate for growing these plants commercially.

Agave leaves also contain some unusual chemicals: some species cause dermatitis, and on others there is a pain-causing chemical on the surface of the spines. The Mexican Indians had a variety of usages for the leaves of different species, including poultices for sores and wounds, soap and fish poisons; *A. lechuguilla* was used to poison arrow tips.

The Mexican Indians also made a drink called pulque from the fermented juice of either *A. americana*, *A. mapisaga* or *A. salmiana*: young flowerheads were cut off to allow the rising sap from the plants to be collected, apparently up to 1000 litres per plant. The species *A. mapisaga* and

Opposite: *Agave victoria reginae*.

A. *angustifolia* are used to make Mescal. It is a distilled liquor of poor quality, made from the fleshy bases of the plants which are baked, fermented and distilled. Another better known and popular drink of good quality made from A. *tequilana* is tequila. The plants have their apical meristem section removed so the remaining base grows bigger and doesn't flower, producing more sugar. These bases are then cut, cooked, mashed and fermented and finally distilled to produce the alcoholic drink used in margaritas.

Some agaves withstand the winters of southern England and southern Europe as well as parts of North America while others are strictly tropical. Most though will tolerate heat, cold, drought and poor soil as long as there is very good drainage. Since most agaves die after flowering, offsets from suckers are important in carrying on the species, but they can also be propagated quite easily from seed.

Agave americana

This species, native to tropical America, but which has naturalised in many areas, grows 2–3 m in height and 4 m wide. Leaves are a greyish green.

Agave americana medio-picta

A yellow variegated form of A. *americana*, with a broad yellow stripe through the middle of the leaves. Variegated forms don't reach the same dimensions as the species, but this is still a bold dramatic plant in the right place. The younger leaves are armed with red teeth and the terminal spines are very sharp.

This page, top: *Agave americana medio-picta*; middle: A. *americana medio-picta alba*; bottom: A. *atrovirens*.

Opposite, top: *Agave angustifolia marginata*; bottom: A. *attenuata*.

Agave americana medio-picta alba

The white variegated form of A. *americana*. Both yellow and white forms can be propagated from offsets.

Agave americana 'variegata'

Another yellow variegation of A. *americana*, but has yellow on the margins of the leaves.

Agave angustifolia marginata

This variegated form of A. *angustifolia* is a very hardy and handsome plant in the garden. It has stiff, regularly set leaves in a rosette reaching 1 m high and 1 m wide. The inflorescence of green to yellow flowers can reach 3–5 m in height. The species grows from Mexico to Costa Rica and copes with coastal habitats and rocky slopes up to 460 m. Propagation from bulbils after flowering or offsets at the base.

Agave atrovirens

This plant is sometimes confused with A. *salmiana* but there is a difference in the texture of the leaves and the fibre. It is a very big agave, reaching 3 m or more high and 3–4 m wide. The leaves can be dark green or glaucous green, they stand up firmly and are deeply channelled with a very heavy sharp terminal spine. The inflorescence can grow to 6 m and bears yellow flowers, the buds tinged with red. This species seems to be extremely variable and will withstand quite severe cold; there are even reports of plants being undamaged after -20°C.

Agave attenuata

This species begins as a stemless plant, but as the rosette of soft broad blue-green leaves ages, the stem grows, and will eventually reach about 1.5 m. It needs protection when temperatures drop below 0°C

and can also suffer leaf damage when humidity reaches high levels in summer. It appears that cell structures break down when transpiration is affected, leaving light patches on the leaves which don't recover. The plant will, however, gradually replace leaves from the central crown. Hail also damages the leaves, leaving pits that can rot if wet weather continues. Despite these problems, A. *attenuata* is one of the most popular agaves for landscaping in New Zealand gardens with its beautiful classical form and attractive colour. Plantlets sometimes grow along the stem and can be removed and grown on.

Agave celsii

This species has soft succulent leaves, the newer ones curving upwards and the older ones spreading downwards. The leaves are light green, varying between apple green and silver grey; there are minute teeth on the margins and the leaf has a weak grey tip. Flowering takes place in late autumn, the flowers being greenish with hints of red or lavender on the inside. This agave benefits from overhead protection in heavy frosts, although it has been known to withstand frosts between -4°C and -11°C in the United States. In the hottest desert areas, protection from the sun is beneficial and the plant needs water in extremely dry conditions. A. *celsii* tends to clump in garden conditions and is a good plant for landscaping as it is attractive in groups. Propagation from offsets or seed.

Top: *Agave chiapensis*; left: *A. celsii*.

Agave chiapensis

This plant has beautiful broad glaucous green leaves edged with small dark teeth and reddish terminal spines. The yellow to green, red- or purple-tinged flowers appear on a 2 m tall spike which tends to curve as it ages. Its name comes from the Mexican state of Chiapas where it grows on the face of limestone outcrops and cliffs. Because this is a warm habitat, the species is likely to be frost tender, but is known to have survived -4°C in Arizona. It is an ideal plant for landscaping, and is propagated from offsets or seed.

Agave decipiens

Deep green leaves, light at the base, are a feature of this agave, which has stems that can grow up to 3 m, usually with a few offsets at ground level. The leaves are about 75–100 cm long spreading from the crown with light coloured teeth on the margins and a firm dark terminal spine. This plant needs good drainage and makes a dramatic statement when planted among rocks. Usually propagated from the numerous bulbils after flowering or from offsets.

Agave filifera

A clumping species that grows to about 60 cm high. Has narrow deep green leaves edged with a few filaments and sharp terminal spines.

Agave franzosinii

A spectacular large species, up to 2.5 m tall and 4.5 m wide. It has very light silver-grey leaves on a wide base, which arch out from the crown and can grow up to 2 m in length, forming a gutter towards the terminal spine. There are brown teeth lining the leaf

Top: *Agave decipiens*; above: *A. franzosinii.*

margins. An enormous inflorescence 8–11 m high produces yellow flowers in autumn. It is interesting that there are no known records of a natural distribution of this species, although it has been planted, particularly in European gardens, for over 100 years. It is thought it could be a close relation of A. *americana*, or a hybrid of unknown origin. The plant needs water if grown in extreme desert areas, but otherwise does well in temperate climates with good drainage. Propagation from offsets or seed.

Agave gigantensis

Named for its widely spaced teeth, this is a stemless plant up to 1 m tall and 1.2 m wide. This species has fewer leaves compared with other agaves, but they are strong, rigid and thick with a horny margin on the upper halves of the grey-green leaves; the widely spaced teeth have unusual shapes and twists. The inflorescence can reach 4–5 m in length and bends with the weight of the flowers, which open a pale cream colour and deepen to yellow as the stamens mature. A. *gigantensis* is endemic to Central Baja, Mexico, where it is quite rare and limited to a largely inaccessible habitat. This plant doesn't produce offsets so seed is the only means of propagation.

Agave guiengola

A medium-sized agave, this plant has glaucous light blue-grey leaves tapering to the tip with a broad gutter narrowing towards the spine. The teeth alternate in size between small and large ones along the leaf margins. The inflorescence is only about 1.8 m long, with pale yellow flowers growing near the base and appearing in spring. A. *guiengola* is said to tolerate more shade than other agaves and tends to create offsets more freely when crowded in a container. With overhead frost protection it can withstand temperatures down to -4°C, but needs irrigation in low desert conditions during summer. Recommended as a stunning ornamental plant. Propagation from offsets or seed.

Below left: Agave gigantensis flowerhead; below: A. guiengola.

Agave kerchovei

A medium-sized, light green agave with a rigid-leaved rosette. The newer leaves are armed with reddish teeth that turn white as they age. It produces a 2–5 m unbranched inflorescence, which is thickly covered in greenish purple small flowers on the upper half; flowers appear in autumn. It grows naturally in semi-arid areas of Mexico, sometimes hybridising with A. *marmorata* which grows in the same areas. Propagation from seed, basal suckers or sometimes bulbils from the inflorescence.

Agave macroculmis

This is a fascinating plant with bright greenish grey leaves edged with pinkish red margins, teeth and terminal spines. The bud imprints make outstanding patterns on the leaves — this plant doesn't need

flowers to be stunning! It sends up a mighty bud, up to 3–5 m long, with bracts on the stem with a panicle of reddish buds opening to yellow flowers. It is thought the bracts protect the buds during snowy winters in the oak and pine forests of Mexico at 2000–2800 m, where it is endemic. A. *macroculmis* requires high rainfall, is cold hardy and tolerates some shade. The flowering shoots are cut off by the Mexican Indians at the asparagus stage and steam cooked, sold in thin slices for a crude sweet and the fibre then spat out on the street! Propagation from seed.

Top left: *Agave kerchovei*; above: *A. macroculmis*.

Agave marmorata

The name 'marmorata' was given for the marble-like colour and texture of the leaves of this species. It isn't one of the largest agaves, reaching only 1.3 m tall by about 3 m wide. It has broad leaves often described as having mamillate margins; the teeth on these projections are yellowish when young and age to red brown. The panicle grows up to 6 m tall, and bears clusters of bright golden-yellow flowers on short laterals in mid-summer. In New Zealand the plant tends to lie to one side, facing north towards the sun. It requires a frost-free situation in cultivation. Propagation from seed only.

Agave oblongata

This has soft broad glaucous blue leaves reminiscent of A. attenuata, which turn up slightly at the tip. The crowns of the plant cluster together in a tight clump bringing good colour to the garden. Spectacular flowerheads appear in summer from the crowns as closely spaced, reddish green buds. As the flowers open, the small pink flower petals roll back tightly, and many pink anthers stand out; these anthers age to white on the lower part of the inflorescence. Offsets from the base are used for propagation.

Agave pachycentra

Very light green leaves are typical of this plant, with a stemless rosette that can bear different coloured teeth and spines on variants of the species; the red brown ones look particularly attractive on the fresh green of the leaves. The inflorescence is not as upright as most agaves, tending to curve outward and then up, with umbels of small yellow flowers. It is a non-fibre agave and inhabits rocky sites in Guatemala. Propagation from seed.

Agave parrasana

This small species has rosettes only 60 cm wide with grey-green leaves, but has large purplish bracts on the 3–4 m flowering stem, which shelters the umbels of buds. A. parrasana comes from the limestone mountains above the desert in Mexico, 1400–2400 m above sea level, living in scrub as well as in pine and oak communities. It is thought to tolerate dry cold to about -6°C. It seldom produces suckers so propagation is best from seed.

Agave parryi

Neat rosettes of an eye-catching, light blue-grey shade, short broad leaves 25–40 cm long and dark teeth plus large black terminal spines, are features of this species. A. parryi can be solitary, but often produces numerous offsets which make a good groundcover. The inflorescence can grow from 3–5 m high, with large umbels of bright yellow flowers from reddish tinted buds; flowering occurs mid- to late summer. This plant is native to the low deserts of Arizona, parts of New Mexico and the Mexican states of Chihuahua and Durango, and is one of

Above: *Agave pachycentra.*

Opposite, top left: *Agave marmorata*; top right: *A. marmorata* flowers; bottom left: *A. parrasana*; bottom right: *A. oblongata.*

the most cold hardy of the agaves, the variety *couesii* withstanding temperatures to -29°C. Other forms such as var. *huachucensis* and var. *truncata* are less cold hardy. In full summer sun in very hot areas the plant does need some water. Propagation from offsets.

Agave parryi var. truncata

Found only in the Mexican state of Durango. The leaves are broader than A. *parryi* and it produces many offsets, a bonus for such an attractive plant.

Agave potatorum

This small-growing species from semi-arid Puebla and Oaxaca in Mexico, is called butterfly agave by the local people. Long red terminal spines show clearly on the light-coloured leaves, described as white to glaucous green; reddish coloured teeth grow from the mamillate prominences. The stem can be 3–6 m tall, and the flowers are light green to yellow with a hint of red on the bracts; they are in either a raceme or a panicle and appear in autumn. This plant is useful as a container specimen because of its compact growth form. It doesn't send out offsets, so propagation is from seed only.

Agave salmiana var. ferox

This is said to be the least hardy of the many forms of A. *salmiana*, but is a spectacular plant with very large glaucous blue-green leaves, thick at the base and gradually getting thinner but broader towards the terminal spine. Plants can reach 1.8 m tall and 3–4 m wide, and the guttered shape has pleasant curves from the broadest part of the leaf to the tip. A 7–8 m tall inflorescence has 15–20 branches with red-tinged buds and yellow flowers. A. *salmiana* grows naturally in a number of areas of Mexico and it is estimated that three quarters of Mexican pulque production comes from this species. The plant has been and still is used extensively in landscape plantings in Europe. Propagation from offsets or seed.

This page, top: *Agave parryi* var. *truncata*; left: A. *salmiana* var. *ferox*.

Opposite, top: *Agave scabra*; bottom left: A. *potatorum*; bottom right: A. *schidigera*.

Agave scabra syn. A. asperrima

This plant has broad grey-green leaves, deeply channelled so they appear almost folded from a distance, with downward pointing teeth on the margins. The inflorescence, which grows to 6 m, is carried on a huge trunk; clusters of yellow flowers appear in summer and are held on horizontal but elegantly curved branches. This agave has a wide distribution, from south-west United States to the Chihuahuan Desert in north Mexico. It grows in very dry areas, 1200–1900 m above sea level, and the juice of this species is used as a sweetener by local Indians. Propagation from offsets or seed.

Agave schidigera

When mature, this plant is about 70 cm wide. It forms a single spherical rosette with many narrow deep green leaves edged with white filaments, and each leaf bears distinct white lines from the bud imprints. The sharp terminal spines are rusty red as they unfurl but bleach to white later. It can produce a raceme about 3.5 m tall with yellow-green flowers in late summer. *A. schidigera* is a useful garden plant for sunny temperate climates as well as containers. Propagation is usually from seed.

Agave shawii ssp. goldmaniana

This sub-species has green leaves, very broad midway and tapering to a long red spine with closely set red teeth on the upper margins. The plant can remain solitary or branch out with several crowns. The inflorescence rises on a stout stem to 5 m tall, branching in the top half with reddish buds that open to yellow flowers. A more heat-tolerant form of *A. shawii*, it is well suited to many areas of landscaping although it has limited frost tolerance. Propagation from basal suckers.

Agave shawii x A. attenuata

A bunching hybrid of attractive glaucous colouring, with leaves featuring attributes of both parents. An excellent plant for landscaping within larger gardens.

Agave stricta

The leaves of *A. stricta* are up to 50 cm long, lightish green tipped with dark reddish brown spines. The inflorescence is a crooked spike growing about 2.5 m long, with red to purple flowers that bloom in summer. It comes from dry limestone hilly areas of Mexico, so is suitable for harsh dry rocky areas. It sends out offsets freely, and colonies of them with their tightly packed leaves and sharp spines in spherical mounds would be difficult to walk through. Interestingly, this agave doesn't die, but divides.

This page, top left: *Agave shawii* ssp. *goldmaniana*; above: *A. stricta* var. *nana*; left: *A. shawii* x *A. attenuata*.

Opposite, top: *Agave titanota*; bottom: *A. vilmoriniana*.

Agave titanota

This plant has distinctive characteristics with light greenish leaves on a single rosette with fascinating teeth and spines showing yellow and red at different stages as they come away from the crown. In its natural habitat A. *titanota* is said to be a glaucous-white colour, but the form in cultivation in New Zealand is light green with a yellowish band down the leaves. The unbranched inflorescence can grow to 3 m with the yellow flowers set against the upper half of the stem. Propagation from offsets or seed.

Agave victoria reginae

A popular small plant (see page 20) for rockeries and containers, this agave grows to about 70 cm wide and is usually solitary, although occasionally offshoots are produced. The hard toothless leaves are a very dark green with clear white lines on both surfaces from bud imprinting. The black terminal spines look almost like a group of penguins facing up to each other. Cream to purple-tinged flowers appear on the upper half of the inflorescence which reaches to 4 m high. This plant is from Mexico where it is now protected after having been in danger of extinction from over-collecting. It is frost tolerant and is propagated from offsets produced around some plants.

Forms of this plant vary considerably in shape and in the amount of bud imprinting displayed, both in their natural habitat and in cultivation, so care is needed in selecting a form that has the best of the attractive attributes that make it so distinctive.

Agave vilmoriniana

This large species that grows to 1.5 m wide, has long curving and recurving bluish green leaves with smooth margins and a flexible terminal spine, hence

its common name octopus agave. The inflorescence is a straight-stemmed raceme reaching 5 m, with yellow to white flowers and many bulbils appearing in the spring; however, it can take up to 15 years to bloom. A. *vilmoriniana* is a cliff-dwelling species from southern Mexico and the plants are said to look like spiders hanging on the walls of deep canyons. It is widely used as a cleaner by Mexican Indians; dried leaves are pounded to make a brush of fibre and when moistened they release saporin, which forms suds for cleaning clothes. This is a beautiful plant, known as one of the 'soft agaves'. Seed is seldom set so propagation is from bulbils.

ALOE

Liliaceae

Aloes are popular plants and have been proven hardy throughout most of the subtropical zone, although some species are known to grow beyond those limits. Those in cultivation come from South Africa, Madagascar and the Middle East, in grassland, scrub and semi-desert areas, but seem tolerant of moving to well-drained areas within arid to subtropical zones. Aloes are not fussy about soil type and most require full sun, but a few exceptions will grow in shade.

Most aloes display a bold structural form, whether as a low-growing rosette, a grass-like plant, a shrub or a tree. They are sometimes classified in groups for their different growth forms or visual attributes, such as tree aloes, single or multi-stemmed, rambling or creeping, stemless, speckled or spotted, dwarf and grass aloes.

The succulent leaves are usually arranged in rosette or spiral formation, and most bear teeth along the edges while some produce these on the upper surface as well, and others have extras on the keel under each leaf. Generally the teeth are not as sharp or as hard as those on agaves, and they don't have a long hard terminal spine on each leaf. Leaf colour varies from deep green to glaucous blue-green shades, and sometimes in hard conditions leaves develop deep orange to red colouration while other species have spots, speckles or lines on the leaf surfaces.

The flowers are often very showy, ranging in colour from greenish yellow through shades of orange to red. The tubular flowers are usually packed densely on spikes or racemes which can be single or in candelabra type inflorescences. Many bloom in winter or spring adding cheerful colour to the garden and offering honey to hungry birds.

The medicinal value of *Aloe vera* and *A. ferox* is well known, the yellow juice near the green leaf surface being used for burns and skin irritations. The cosmetic industry uses aloe gel, the thick jelly-like substance found within the leaves, as a base for hair and skin care products. In the West Indies, East Africa and parts of India and China, *A. vera* is cultivated as a crop for aloe gel.

Aloes can be propagated from seed, from divisions taken off the clumping varieties, or from well-dried stem cuttings.

Above: *Aloe arborescens* variegated.

Opposite: *Aloe polyphylla*.

Aloe arborescens

A very bushy plant growing to about 2 m and equally as wide, it is said to be the most widely cultivated aloe in the world. Rosettes of the blue-green foliage (called truncheons when they have a stem) have slightly recurved leaves edged with teeth. Orange tubular flowers appear in winter to make a bright display and are held high above the leaves on a tapering inflorescence. This aloe hybridises freely with other species and grows over extensive coastal areas of South Africa. When grown as a hedge from truncheons or basal crowns in dry, sandy windswept areas, it makes an animal-proof windbreak and hedge. The jelly-like sap can be used as first aid treatment on burns and abrasions.

Aloe arborescens variegated

This plant has attractive yellow striping on the leaves.

Aloe aristata

From South Africa, this small grower clumps, and the tuberculate green leaves with white spots reach about 14 cm in cultivation. A clump can produce a number of inflorescences about 35 cm high, with racemes of many tubular light reddish orange flowers in early summer. In harsh conditions the leaves are narrow and curved, but in better cond-itions or cultivated areas they are wider and thicker.

Left and below: *Aloe arborescens*; bottom: *A. aristata*.

Aloe barbarae
(syn. A. bainesii)

This is the tallest tree aloe, originally from South Africa, which grows up to 18 m with a trunk diameter of 3 m. The dark green leaves are deeply channelled and recurved with small whitish teeth. It naturally has many branches, but can be pruned to any desired form in cultivation. The salmon to orange flowers are formed on a branched inflorescence. *A. barbarae* is frost tender when young.

Right: *Aloe barbarae* flowers; below: *A. barberae* after pruning.

Aloe barbadensis
(syn. A. vera)

A grey-leaved aloe that gradually spreads from side shoots to form a dense clump. It was originally from North Africa or the Middle East, but spread to the Mediterranean centuries ago, and since being introduced to central North America has run wild in many areas. The upright leaves, about 30 cm, are used medicinally and for cosmetics. Tall narrow spikes of yellow or orange flowers bloom above the foliage.

Aloe berhana

The broad deep green leaves on rosettes, reaching almost 2 m in diameter, and branching inflorescences up to 2 m with conical heads of red flowers, make this a very showy aloe.

Aloe branddraaiensis

A South African aloe, named after the Branddraai district where it was first collected, this plant forms small clumps from suckers. In shady areas the leaves don't colour much, but when under stress the greenish red leaves turn brown and the white spots arranged in rows show up more clearly. Sharp brown teeth arm the margins, and inflorescences with several branches carry many short heads of coral-red tubular flowers in winter.

Aloe capitata var. capitata

From Madagascar, this is generally a solitary stemless plant. It has greenish red leaves edged with red thorns. The flowers appear in winter and are yellow, tubular and in dense short clusters on a branching inflorescence. An attractive plant for the dry garden.

This page, top left: *Aloe branddraaiensis*; top right: A. *capitata* var. *capitata* flowers; above: A. *capitata* var. *capitata*.

Opposite, top: *Aloe barbadensis*; bottom: A. *berhana*.

Aloe comosa

From a very dry area in eastern Cape Province, South Africa, this single-stemmed plant grows to 2 m high. The flowerheads are dull pink, fading to white; they arise from the crown and are very tall and slender, sometimes to nearly 3 m long. The old leaves are persistent on this plant.

Aloe cooperi

A grassland species with deep green leaves that grow to about 70 cm, A. cooperi grows in two ranks with white-spotted bases. The beautiful waxy flowers, orange and green, are formed in a cone-shaped inflorescence and stand 1 m or more above the leaves; flowers appear in late summer to early autumn. In their homeland of eastern Cape Province, South Africa, they are said to grow in either dry rocky or wet marshy areas, an unusual contrast of habitats.

This page, top left: *Aloe comosa*; top right: A. *cooperi* flowers; above: A. *cooperi*.

Opposite, top: *Aloe dichotoma*; bottom: A. *distans*.

Aloe dichotoma

From arid and rocky areas of eastern South Africa, this tree aloe has many forked branches, and a tight head of grey-green leaves. The bark of the tree is rough with razor sharp edges and the trunks can be almost cone shaped. Yellow flowers are borne on a short inflorescence. Quiver tree is its common name as the hollow stems were used for making quivers by the people of Namibia.

Aloe distans

Another South African aloe, but this one is confined to a coastal belt. It is a sprawling plant, sometimes rooting where it lies and making a clump. The formal rosettes consist of broad glaucous green leaves up to 15 cm long, usually with several white spots on both upper and lower surfaces, and distinctive yellow teeth on the margins. A branched inflorescence has pendent and densely packed tubular flowers in a dull scarlet colour; the flowerheads are somewhat flattened.

Aloe ferox

A tall-stemmed plant growing up to 5 m, with a single crown and persistent old leaves on the trunk. The leaves form a dense rosette and are up to 1 m long, broad at the base, a dull reddish green with many scattered spines on the upper surface; the margins are armed with large sharp reddish teeth. The inflorescence has 5–8 erect racemes, with densely packed, bright scarlet flowers on them. This aloe is of medicinal importance in South Africa as a purgative drug called 'Cape Aloes' and has been commercially used for over 200 years. The juice of A. *ferox* is collected from leaves stacked with the cut ends over a skin bowl and the juice boiled until evaporated, leaving a hard dry substance.

Aloe greenii

A stoloniferous plant that in its natural habitat grows mainly among bushes in valleys where temperatures reach the high thirties in summer. The long tapering leaves are dark green and attractively marked with spots in transverse bands, looking better in cultivation than in the wild. The inflorescence is very tall, over 1 m high, and branched from halfway up; flowers appear from late summer to early autumn and are a dull pink.

This page, above: Aloe greenii; left: A. *ferox*.

Opposite, top: Aloe humilis; bottom: A. *juvenna*.

Aloe humilis

Commonly known as the dwarf hedgehog aloe, this is a clumping plant that quickly doubles its size in cultivation. The glaucous leaves are slightly incurved, sometimes pinkish on the tips, and have a few tubercles and prickles on the lower surface and white teeth on the margins. The spring flowers are scarlet with yellow tips and loosely spaced on the stem, which grows up to 35 cm high. *A. humilis* has been in cultivation a long time and was one of the species grown in the Dutch East India Company's garden in Capetown, South Africa, in 1695.

Aloe juvenna

This is a many-branched clumping dwarf aloe. The foliage is a light bright green colour with many white spots and white teeth. Flowering stems are up to 30 cm long with a single spike of tubular green-tipped red flowers. It is an attractive rock garden plant, but with limited cold tolerance.

Aloe karasbergensis

A solitary plant with light grey-green leaves without teeth, but with darker longitudinal lines. The many-branched inflorescence, about 75 cm in length, has short terminal racemes of evenly spread tubular pink to red flowers. This plant always attracts attention in the garden.

Aloe laeta

A small grower, this aloe only reaches about 30 cm in height. It has upright glaucous leaves with numerous small pink teeth on the margins. The branched inflorescence rises from the centre of the crown, and bears coral-red flowers about 20 cm above the foliage.

This page: *Aloe mutans.*

Opposite, top left: *Aloe karasbergensis*; top right: *A. mitriformis*; bottom: *A. laeta.*

Aloe mitriformis

A South African aloe that appears to be a very variable species. It is of sprawling growth habit but can make quite dense clumps in its natural habitat, which receives up to 750 mm of rain per year with a little humidity. The plant flowers in summer, with some forms bearing capitate racemes and others conical, up to 50 cm high and scarlet to pink in colour.

Aloe mutans

This stemless suckering South African aloe has deep green leaves with numerous dull white spots in irregular transverse bands. The older leaves are untidy in the natural habitat as they die back from the ends in the heat of a hot bare plain of red sand. It has a branching stem reaching 90 cm, and narrow racemes with spring flowers; flowers are strawberry pink to orange yellow, the yellow being accentuated after pollination.

Aloe peglarae

The species was found in Transvaal, South Africa, in 1903 by Alice Pegler. A small plant reaching only 30 cm, it grows naturally in rocky, sunny well-drained areas. It has strongly incurved glaucous blue-green leaves, armed with sharp incurved spines on the margins and upper leaf surfaces, and a sharp terminal spine. It bears a single inflorescence with closely packed orange turning to yellow, tubular flowers; blooms appear in late winter. Photographs of the species in its natural habitat show its fascinating shape, when the leaves turn in so strongly that they touch the base of the single candle-like inflorescence.

This page, left: *Aloe plicatilis*; below: *A. peglarae*.

Opposite, top: *Aloe polyphylla* flowers; bottom: *A. pluridens*.

Aloe plicatilis

Commonly called the fan aloe, because the fans of leaves divide at the top to make further branches, large specimens can reach 4–5 m high. The red flowers stand out on single inflorescences in spring. In 1695 Superintendent Oldenland, of the Dutch East India Company Garden at Capetown, South Africa, named this plant *Aloe african arborescens montana non spinosa, longissimo, plicatili, flore rubra* — the modern botanical name is much easier for all concerned! *A. plicatilis* grows naturally in mountainous areas where the rainfall is 600–1200 mm per year, and is endemic to a small area in the Western Cape mountains of South Africa. This plant is admired in gardens for its unusual form.

Aloe pluridens

A tall plant, reaching 3–4 m, either single-stemmed or branched, *A. pluridens* is considered close to *A. arborescens* in type, but has longer narrower leaves, pale green with more and smaller teeth. It has orange-red flowers but not in such abundance as the other species. It grows naturally in hot bushy areas where there is no frost.

Aloe polyphylla

This is one of the rarer aloes and the stemless rosette's spiralling growth form is quite unique. Plants reach about 50 cm high and up to 80 cm wide, and occur naturally on mountain slopes in Lesotho, about 2500–2600 m above sea level so are often covered in snow. They are solitary plants, although they do grow in groups. Light-coloured teeth edge the light green leaves, which have a spine, often reddish coloured at the tip; there is an offset keel ridge under each leaf. The inflorescence is branched from low down, with short heads of densely packed, pale reddish flowers, which appear in late spring to early summer. *A. polyphylla* was first discovered in 1915 but not written up botanically and published with photos until 1934. It always attracts attention as a garden specimen. It only occasionally divides into another crown, so is usually propagated from seed.

This page, top: *Aloe prinslooi*; above left: A. *rauhii*; above right: A. *reitzii*.

Opposite, top: *Aloe speciosa*; bottom: A. *'rookappie'*.

Aloe prinslooi

An easily cultivated species from Natal, South Africa, where winters are dry and cold, and summer has more than 800 mm of rain. The plants are usually solitary with broad deep green leaves, decorated with bands of oblong greenish white spots, and armed with sharp curved reddish teeth. Flowering occurs in cultivation in winter or sometimes summer, and the whitish green turning to deep shell-pink flowers are held in short racemes on a branched inflorescence reaching up to 60 cm high.

Aloe rauhii

A very small plant, with green leaves that turn reddish on the ends and their entire surface speckled with dull white oblong spots. It is a clumping plant suited to container growing or a rockery.

Aloe reitzii

This species from a small area of Transvaal, South Africa, has light blue-green upright leaves in rosettes up to 90 cm in diameter. The bright red flowers appearing in late summer make this an attractive species to grow. Its natural habitat is on rocky slopes.

Aloe 'rookappie'

This aloe has an attractive rosette of green to reddish leaves, with a few small whitish streaks running down them, and with red teeth. The branched inflorescence bears flat-topped racemes of deep red to orange flowers, yellow tipped, in the spring.

Aloe speciosa

A tall single-stemmed aloe that can reach 6 m when grown in tall bush, but is often branched and shorter when grown in the open. The rosette of leaves often tilts sideways and leaf formation is not as regular as some aloes, often twisting at odd angles. The greenish grey leaves are armed with very small reddish teeth while the leaf margin has a narrow reddish edge; the old leaves will persist on the trunk. The several inflorescences are unbranched and grow to 50 cm, producing greenish orange flowers in spring, the orange colour coming from the anthers as they extend.

Aloe striata

One of the most popular cultivated species of aloe, this was grown at Kew Gardens, London, prior to 1795, when it was known as the streaked aloe. Today it is more commonly called the coral aloe because of the flower colour. The light blue-green leaves streaked with a darker green, have a narrow pinkish border and smooth leaf margins with no teeth. The branched inflorescence bears heads of tubular coral-red flowers in spring. There can be variations in both the leaf markings and the shape of the flower racemes in this species but the plants do well in cultivation, usually as a single crown which tends to lean over. Prolonged cold wet conditions can cause rot.

Aloe striatula

A rather untidy branching plant found on mountain tops in South Africa, it does well in cultivation. Narrow recurving, glossy dark green leaves with very small teeth form rosettes on top of stems that can reach over 1 m. The yellow-green flowers are formed on a single-stemmed narrow spike, and bloom in early summer.

Aloe tenuior

This semi-scrambling plant from South Africa grows through other shrubs for support in the wild. The plant will spread into a large stand if allowed. Bright yellow flowers in narrow spears appear on thin stems throughout the year.

Aloe thompsoniae

This aloe grows to about 20 cm high, and its natural habitat is misty, drizzly mountain areas about 1800 m above sea level with high rainfall, usually 2100 mm a year. The green soft-leaved plant has unusually bright orange flowers with yellow tips that stand up to 30 cm high. It is an ideal plant for a rockery or container growing, flowering over a long period from late spring through summer. Planted in hot, very dry conditions it is known to die, not surprisingly given its natural habitat, but given soil with good drainage in a temperate climate this little aloe will increase rapidly.

Aloe thraskii

This single-stemmed aloe grows up to 2 m high, and is naturally a coastal plant, being found growing in pure sand in Natal. It has strongly recurved leaves but the old ones persist on the trunk. Two or three inflorescences are produced on each plant, branching to carry spectacular cylindrical upright racemes of yellow flowers that appear orange as the stamens emerge; masses of bees enjoy the honey from this winter-blooming plant. A stand of this aloe in bloom against the sea is a great sight.

This page: *Aloe thraskii*.

Opposite, top left: *Aloe striata*; top right: A. *striatula*; bottom left: A. *tenuior*; bottom right: A. *thompsoniae*.

Aloe ukambensis

A handsome plant with dark green leaves heavily tinged red and bearing red teeth on the margins. The leaves are broad at the base, gradually tapering and turning inwards.

Aloe vaombe

This aloe from Madagascar grows naturally as a solitary plant of 2–3 m. It has downward-curving channelled leaves, broad at the base, with white teeth. The 2–4 branched inflorescences that appear simultaneously have orange-red curved tubular flowers. Propagation from seed.

Aloe variegata

A small stemless aloe with speckled dark green leaves, the spotting is in transverse bands. The rosettes are made up of leaves arranged in three rows that grow up to 15 cm in length. The unbranched inflorescence reaches about 30 cm in height, with red to pink flowers that bloom in spring. This species is intolerant of over-watering, the base rotting in wet conditions, but makes an interesting addition to container collections. Propagation is from suckers which arise quite freely when the plant is doing well.

Top: *Aloe vaombe*; above: *A. variegata*.

ALOINOPSIS

Aizoaceae

Aloinopsis are interesting small fleshy plants from the dry areas of Cape Province, South Africa. They add variety to indoor collections of small plants unsuited to regular rainfall. Propagate from seed or divisions.

Aloinopsis malcherbei

Rounded dark green leaves with white tubercles over the outer surfaces and upper edges form rosettes about 4 cm across, and add interest to this small plant.

Aloinopsis rubrolineata

Deep green flattish leaves about 3 cm long are covered in very small light green tubercles, which add texture.

Top: *Aloinopsis rubrolineata*; above: *A. malcherbei*.

Aloinopsis schoonesii

A dense cluster of small thick green leaves covered in tiny dark green dots, the leaves 3 cm long with partially flattened tops.

Aloinopsis setifara

This plant has thick irregular-shaped leaves, 2–3 cm long, with partially flattened tops covered in white tubercles.

Top: *Aloinopsis schoonesii*;
left: *A. setifera*.

APTENIA

Aizoaceae

This drought-resistant genus is native to the harsh coastal deserts of eastern South Africa. It is a groundcovering succulent with small fleshy bright green leaves and little daisy-like flowers, brightly coloured.

Aptenia cordifolia 'Baby Sun Rose'

This creeper has naturalised in coastal desert areas in other parts of the world. The fleshy fresh green 2.5 cm leaves are covered with glands which go grey as the leaves age. The rose-purple flowers are 1 cm in diameter. Propagates easily from cuttings or seed.

Above: *Aptenia cordifolia.*

ARGYRODERMA

Aizoaceae

Argyroderma, one of the so-called pebble plants, are from Cape Province, South Africa. These fascinating plants have one pair of very rounded, almost globular, smooth leaves up to 2 cm long, with a flat inner surface where the two leaf faces meet. The flower is a single daisy type, which appears between the leaves with little or no stem. This is a collectors' plant, which demands perfect drainage. Propagation is from seed.

Argyroderma pearsonii

This species clearly shows the fat fleshy leaves typical of the genus, in a very pale grey.

Above: *Argyroderma pearsonii.*

BEAUCARNEA

Agavaceae

These shrubs with a bulbous water-storing base are native to dry areas of Texas and Mexico. They're often grown as container plants and can be kept in containers for some years, the size and weight for handling becoming a problem eventually. These are not plants that can be pruned in any way, so need to be left alone to form their own special and distinctive shape, growing up to 9 m tall with a base of at least 2 m in diameter. By this time the tree has branched at the top; although in conditions wetter than their natural habitat some plants will branch when quite young. Side shoots can be rubbed off if a clean-stemmed specimen is preferred. It has narrow leaves like a dense tuft of coarse grass, spreading from the crown of the plant. Very tiny cream flowers are produced by old plants in a plume up to 80 cm long.

Plants are happy in full sun but will tolerate semi-shade. Propagation from seed.

Beaucarnea recurvata (syn. Nolina)

Commonly known as the ponytail palm. Attractive during its early years as a single-stemmed plant with a bulbous base, most of which is above ground and covered in a soft bark. The leaves form a recurving green 'fountain' at the top and are about 1 m long and 2 cm wide with slightly rough edges; lower leaves can easily be pulled off when they age and discolour. Although the bulbous base appears hard, it is actually quite soft so care is necessary when repotting or handling, as bruising can cause rot to form in the white flesh within. *B. recurvata* enjoys full sun and well-drained soil. Some moisture is needed for newly planted specimens in hot dry conditions, but there is said to be enough moisture stored in mature plants to last a year. Mature plants are noted for withstanding temperatures below freezing point, but care is needed with young plants both in the ground and containers.

Beaucarnea stricta

Has much stiffer leaves than *B. recurvata*, 60 cm long, and many remain erect in the crown of the plant; they are also bluer in colour. The base of *B. stricta* is not quite as bulbous as the other species, and tends to taper up the trunk.

Left: *Beaucarnea recurvata.*

BESCHORNERIA

Amaryllidaceae

This genus, native to Mexico, has 10 species, all with stemless rosettes and strap-like leaves. They are considered half hardy and need full sun with a well-drained soil, very useful for landscaping sunny banks. Propagation from offsets at the base of mature plants.

Beschorneria toneliana

This plant has shiny green strap-like leaves growing to 60 cm, and an exciting branched inflorescence reaching 1.5 m in length, with candy-red flowers.

Beschorneria yuccoides

This species has a very large rosette with 20 or more strap-like leaves up to 90 cm long and 10 cm wide; the leaves are glaucous blue-green with rough margins and undersides. The pink flower stems, growing up to 2 m long, tend to lean over and carry pendent green flowers with pink bracts. B. yuccoides favours warm dry conditions, and will set seed when two or more plants flower in close proximity. Seedlings will flower in their third season.

Beschorneria yuccoides variegata

A handsome form with bold creamy yellow variegation and a bunching growth habit.

Right: *Carpobrotus edulis.*

CARPOBROTUS

Aizoaceae

Carpobrotus are originally from South Africa but have naturalised in many other parts of the world. They are mat-forming perennial succulents with triangular fleshy green leaves, and bear daisy-like shining flowers in the sun. Propagation is easy from cuttings.

Carpobrotus edulis

Commonly known as the Hottentot fig, this strong creeping branching succulent is often used as a sand binder on beaches and even against roads in many countries. The leaves are 3-sided, and the large shining silky flowers up to 10 cm across change from yellow to pinkish orange as they age in the sun. The large fruits are said to be edible.

COLLETIA

Rhamnaceae

An unusual shrub with short thick blue-grey leaves, their widest part against the stem, joining a similar leaf opposite; the next pair of leaves sits very closely to the previous pair, facing the opposite direction. Each leaf is actually a flattened stem, terminating in a short spine with hundreds of minute white bell-shaped flowers emerging under and on the leaves and against the stems in late summer. Propagation from cuttings.

Colletia paradoxa

This plant with its fascinating arrangement of leaves comes from Brazil and Uruguay, and the scent of vanilla from the thousands of small flowers set against the leaves and stems is wonderful.

Below: *Colletia paradoxa.*

CONOPHYTUM

Aizoaceae

This large group of succulents has over 200 species, and grows naturally in Cape Province and Namaqualand, South Africa. They are mostly stemless dwarf plants with each shoot formed by two united fleshy leaves of an inverted cone shape with a fissure across the upper surface. The upper surface of some species is speckled with dots, usually on a background of green, grey, bluish or reddish colour. The single flower grows out from the division in the leaves in autumn and can be yellow, orange, pink, white or purple.

Plants generally grow in clumps, increasing by dividing in two; the previous season's leaves dry up in spring and new ones emerge from beneath these.

These plants need a free-draining soil mix and indoor conditions in most areas, and because the roots don't absorb moisture until the new leaves have grown each season, don't water plants in early summer. Propagate from cuttings with part of the stem included.

Conophytum crassum

Vertically flattened leaves, typical of this species, are about 3 cm long and green grey with reddish tips. Flowers are yellow.

Conophytum ornatum

Light grey-green leaves, 2 cm long, are almost totally joined into flattened domes.

Conophytum truncatum

Small light blue-grey leaves, 2–3 cm long, are dotted with a deeper shade with a light red line running over the edges and apex. Flowers are yellow.

Conophytum violaeiflorum

Flattened leaves, 2 cm long, are in upright pairs with a reddish line over the top. Flowers are orange.

Top left: *Conophytum ornatum*; above: *C. truncatum*; below: *C. crassum*.

COTYLEDON

Crassulaceae

Cotyledons are often bushy plants, somewhat hardier than most of the crassula family and come from South Africa, Namibia, Abyssinia and the Middle East. The more commonly cultivated forms usually grow to less than 1 m, although one deciduous species, *Cotyledon paniculata*, grows up to 3 m with thick stems.

Their leaves can be broad, roundish, spoon shaped or cylindrical, smooth, wavy edged, polished, thick with bloom or hairy. Leaf colours vary from white to reddish green and are glaucous, some having a red edge.

Cotyledons have very pretty bell-shaped flowers, usually held in an umbel on a thin stem well above the foliage. The flower stem rises from the centre of the leaf growth, separating them from echeverias which send out flower stems from the sides of the plants. Flowers range in colour from yellow to red and greenish tints.

These easy-to-grow succulents are extremely useful and showy for the garden and containers and some will even naturalise in quite cold areas. Most prefer full sun, but partial shade is best for the smaller-growing species. Established plants can be pruned to keep the desired shape or level.

Most of the cotyledons in cultivation are cultivars, the larger-leaved forms coming from *C. orbiculata*, and the naming of these has been somewhat confusing, but I have endeavoured to present the latest listing for these. Propagation from pieces or seed.

Cotyledon mucronata 'Silver Crown' (formerly *C. undulata*)

The silver-white rounded opposite leaves of this plant have a distinctive crimped edge that is quite unusual, but unfortunately the plant is rather difficult to grow in cultivation. Flowers are orange.

Cotyledon orbiculata var. orbiculata (now includes *C. macrantha*)

This species is bushy, up to about 75 cm wide in established plantings. It makes an eye-catching display

planted in a group; it is widely grown outdoors for its outstanding leaf colour and form as well as the attractive flowers. The leaves can be either green with a red edge or silver white with a faint red edge, and are almost a flattened spoon shape with a hint of a point at the apex. Salmon-pink flowers are held high above the foliage; they are the typical bell shape of this genus, and have a beautiful satiny texture.

Cotyledon orbiculata 'Elk Horns'

This forms a compact attractive bush about 60 cm high. It bears cylindrical glaucous silver leaves about 10 cm long as a young plant, but gradually produces the flattened and divided terminals, hence its name 'Elk Horns'. Needs a free-draining sunny situation.

This page, above and top right: *Cotyledon orbiculata* var. *orbiculata*; right: *C. orbiculata* 'Elk Horns'.

Opposite: *Cotyledon orbiculata* var. *orbiculata*.

Cotyledon tomentosa ssp. *ladismithiensis*

This plant will grow to about 30 cm high, with thick green hairy leaves showing several interesting red teeth on the upper margins. The orange pendent flowers grow 8–10 to a stem. There is also a rare variegated form of this plant. Often treated as an indoor plant because it prefers partial shade, but can be grown successfully in a suitable outdoor area.

Cotyledon orbiculata 'Silver Waves'

This form is attractive for its very white wavy leaves that add contrast in the garden or interest to container-grown succulents in other colours. The flowers, similar to C. *orbiculata*, are not held up as firmly. It has a tendency to sprawl as it ages and this is ideal in some garden situations, and for container use where the spreading clusters of white foliage can soften the harsh look of the container.

Above: *Cotyledon orbiculata* 'Silver Waves'; top right and right: C. *tomentosa* ssp. *ladismithiensis* and variegated form.

CRASSULA

Crassulaceae

There are about 190 species in this large genus, including annuals, perennials, shrubs and semi-aquatic plants. Most species are native to South Africa, but others come from tropical Africa, Madagascar, the Middle East and Europe.

Features that make this group of plants popular range from the brilliant flower colour of some species, to the red leaves of others or the perfection of their arrangement.

Growth habits vary from groundcover forms to the tree-like *Crassula arborescens*, up to 4 m high.

The small amphibious to semi-aquatic species from New Zealand, C. *helmslii*, was introduced to Britain as an aquarium plant and has been released into waterways and even been taken to North America, and is now considered a pest where it clogs waterways.

There are now a number of crassula cultivars available, as well as hybrids, many of which were created by enthusiasts during and after the 1940s.

Propagation is usually from cuttings or basal divisions.

Crassula albiflora
(syn. C. dejecta)

In hot dry situations this low-growing plant, up to 45 cm high, is very useful as a colourful filler or groundcover. When planted in poor soil and dry conditions the foliage, normally red tipped, turns a brilliant red. The small white flowers are carried in clusters on stems above the foliage in autumn.

Crassula arborescens

Commonly called the silver jade plant, this is a dense-growing thick-stemmed plant which can become tree-like with a trunk up to 4 m high. It is very slow growing, however, and excellent in pots and dry gardens, where the rounded, red-edged glaucous leaves are very compact and tidy. It produces small starry pink or white flowers in spring.

Above: *Crassula arborescens*; left: *C. albiflora*.

Crassula coccinea 'Flame'

Believed to be a hybrid, this branching plant has pointed light yellow-green leaves in spring that turn a bright coppery red during autumn. At the same time the stems suddenly grow upwards, reaching about 40 cm, with a terminal cluster of minute cream flowers in each leaf axel. The plant becomes straggly after flowering so pruning is necessary to promote further basal growth. Propagate from basal growth or stems.

Crassula coccinea 'Garden Coral'

This produces stems up to 30 cm high, with opposite and alternating small thin green leaves very closely spaced, so that from above there are four even rows. They lead up to the terminal cluster of bright red tubular flowers that appear in summer. The plant is uninteresting after flowering so pruning back as the flowers fade to promote new growth is important. New plants can be grown from cuttings.

Crassula deceptor

A very small grey-speckled plant with thick overlapping leaves in short columns. Thin stems taller than the plant bear tiny whitish flowers. This plant is seen in indoor collections rather than outdoors.

Crassula 'Green Pagoda'

A small plant growing to about 10 cm high, with upright columns of tiered and alternate 7 mm-wide green leaves, sometimes with a very narrow red edge. When growing well, branches will sometimes form on the columns. Terminal clusters of small flowers opening white and deepening to a pretty pink are attractive.

Crassula mesembrianthemopsis

This is a very small plant for such a long name! This crassula forms a tight mound of overlapping crowns of small grey-green flat-topped leaves, has small white flowers and is sought after by collectors for indoor collections.

Crassula 'Morgan's Beauty'

An indoor hybrid with thick irregular wedge-shaped blue-grey leaves in a tight mound, which produces unexpected clusters of long-lasting and beautiful salmon-pink flowers. The plant was raised by Dr Meredith Morgan of California by crossing C. mesembrianthemopsis with C. falcata. Spider mites enjoy this plant, hiding between the tightly packed leaves.

This page: Crassula coccinea 'Flame'.

Opposite, top left: Crassula deceptor; top right:
C. mesembrianthemopsis; bottom: C. 'Morgan's Beauty'.

Crassula ovata
(syns. C. argentea, C. portulacea, C. oblique)

This is the well-known jade plant, which grows to a dense bushy plant up to 3 m high. It has shiny green leaves often with a red edge. Small pinkish white clusters of flowers are showy in winter.

This page, left and below: *Crassula ovata* syn. *portulacea*.

Opposite, top left: *Crassula ovata* 'Gollum'; top right: *C. ovata* tricolor; bottom: *C. ovata* variegata.

Crassula ovata 'Gollum'

This plant is of mounding growth and can reach 1 m high. It has soft fleshy incurved green leaves, about 50 cm long, rolled or 'quilled' to a point where they appear tubular; grown in good light, the rounded edges of the leaves will be bright red. Usually grown indoors.

Crassula ovata 'Hobbit'

This cultivar is very similar to C. *ovata* 'Gollum', but does not show off the quilled leaf ends as well.

Crassula ovata tricolor
(formerly C. portulacea)

This is a dense bushy small-leaved shrub that reaches 1 m or more in height. It is a golden form of C. *ovata* with thick red stems and yellow leaves on all the newer growth.

Crassula ovata variegata

An ideal container plant, the variegated leaves are at their best in semi-shade.

Crassula perfoliata var. falcata
(syn. C. falcata)

Sometimes called the propeller plant because of its very thick, tapering light blue-grey leaves that twist slightly like a propeller. The spectacular red flowers grow in large clusters above the foliage. Unfortunately, this plant often becomes straggly and is sometimes a target for spider mites that spoil the colour of the foliage.

Crassula perforata
(formerly C. perfossa)

This plant's common name is string of buttons, and has very symmetrical foliage, the thick leaves being joined in pairs right round the stem. A horny edge can be felt on the margins of the leaves, but these edges won't colour unless grown outdoors. A terminal spike of small white flowers appears in late autumn, and after flowering the plants need cutting back to keep compact. Propagation from stem cuttings.

This page, top: *Crassula perfoliata* var. *falcata*; above: *C. perforata*.

Opposite, top and bottom: *Crassula pubescens* ssp. *radicans*.

Crassula pubescens ssp. radicans

Can be used as a groundcover as it grows to about 20 cm in height. Given enough moisture the small crowded leaves are green, but as drier and hotter conditions prevail the leaves turn bright red. Small umbels of tiny white flowers top thin stems above the leaves in spring.

Crassula rosularis

This species has a rosette of thin strap-shaped leaves, 10–15 mm wide and about 6 cm long, in a deep reddish green colour. An upright inflorescence with small clusters of tiny white flowers grows from the centre of the rosette.

Crassula tetragona

This hardy upright tree-like plant grows to about 40 cm, with narrow cylindrical glossy green leaves arranged opposite each other. Terminal clusters of tiny white flowers appear in spring.

DASYLIRION

Liliaceae

These unusual grass trees come from southern United States and northern South America, and make outstanding 'spiky balls' in warm dry areas. The rosette forms are made up from hundreds of stiff sharp-pointed leaves, not pleasant to walk into as they stand about 3 m high and 3 m wide, and some species have infloresences up to 5 m long.

Dasylirion longissimum

The Mexican grass tree or junquillo is a stemless xerophyte. A dense bundle of stiffly erect olive-green leaves with terminal spines come from the swollen base. Small creamy yellow flowers are massed on a single upright inflorescence.

Dasylirion wheeleri

Arizona, Texas and Mexico are home to this plant, sometimes called a desert spoon. It has a dense rosette of narrow flexuous ribbed leaves with terminal and marginal spines that shine in the light. An excellent plant for a dry area.

Top left: *Dasylirion* in flower; top right: *D. wheeleri*; above: *D. longissimum*.

DELOSPERMA

Aizoaceae

These are mat-forming or low shrubby plants from South Africa. They have varying shaped small succulent greyish leaves, and shiny daisy-like flowers; flower colours range from reddish purple to pink, white and yellow. This plant propagates easily from cuttings.

Delosperma lehmannii

A groundcovering plant with compact thick-keeled grey-green 1 cm long leaves and cream flowers.

DINTERANTHUS

Aizoaceae

These plants from Namibia have pale grey globular leaves each about 1 cm thick and 3 cm long, set in pairs with flat surfaces facing each other. The yellow flower is produced on a stem. Propagation from seed.

Dinteranthus wilmotianus

This small pale grey pebble plant is an interesting succulent to add to a collection of indoor plants that need a little watering in summer and almost total neglect during the winter.

Left: *Delosperma lehmannii.*

Above: *Dinteranthus wilmotianus.*

DIOSCOREA

Dioscoreaceae

These weird plants from South Africa grow a caudex at the base and produce thin stems of climbing vines from the centre; it takes some years to develop a large caudex. Propagation from seed.

Dioscorea elephantipes

Common names for this plant are elephant's foot or Hottentot bread. The interesting-looking base forms corrugated angled bark knobs as it grows, eventually reaching about 1 m in diameter. It sends up a few stems that grow into vines, twining to 2 m or more if support is available, with deciduous green heart-shaped leaves. Small greenish yellow flowers are formed, but the plants are dioecious, or single sexed.

Right and below: *Dioscorea elephantipes.*

DISPHYMA

Aizoaceae

Commonly called ice plants, these New Zealand natives are very attractive in flower, and useful as trailing plants over banks in dry windy areas. They are very much at home in coastal sand and cliff areas. Propagation from cuttings.

Disphyma australe

A coastal ice plant, which trails over banks and cliffs. The 2–4 cm wide flowers range from white to pink.

Disphyma papillatum

From the Chatham Islands, this is a small linear-leaved trailing ice plant, with 2–4 cm wide white, pink or purple flowers.

Above: *Disphyma papillatum.*

DRACAENA

Liliaceae

Dracaenas, from equatorial Asia and Africa, are strap-leaved trees or shrubs frequently used for landscaping and as indoor plants. The smaller-growing species with cane-like stems are preferred as indoor plants and can be cut back to near ground level in spring. They will grow in full sun and tolerate shade, but are frost tender. Propagation from seed or stem cuttings.

Dracaena deremensis 'Warneckei'

This species from tropical Africa is generally grown as a house plant. The strap-like foliage spreads from the crown of the cane, which can grow to several metres high if not cut back to ground level occasionally. From a green leaf base this one has interesting creamy white streaks in the centre, a white band each side and green margins.

Top left: *Dracaena draco* flowers; above: *D. draco* berries.

Dracaena draco

From the Canary Islands, this species is known as the dragon tree because of the red sap that can flow from an injury. The roots are also red. These trees can reach 20 m high, with a trunk up to 4.5 m in diameter, and are decorative as young plants with their sword-like fleshy glaucous green leaves with a fine red margin. Banded patterns form on the trunk as it gets taller and it will eventually have many branches leading to a flattish crown. The inflorescence from the rosette of leaves is branched, bearing numerous small cream flowers; later green berries form on the inflorescence, these turn bright orange as they mature. Aerial roots formed at the base of older trees are impressive.

Dracaena marginata 'Tricolor'

One of the small indoor or tropical house growers with very effective bands of colour in the narrow leaves.

Above: *Dracaena draco* trunks.

DROSANTHEMUM

Aizoaceae

This genus from South Africa is another from the ice plant group, with small fleshy 2 cm leaves and masses of bright shiny flowers. They are extremely heat tolerant but do enjoy some moisture. Propagate from cuttings.

Drosanthemum speciosum
A narrow-leaved bushy perennial with bright orange-red and yellow daisy-like flowers.

Left: *Drosanthemum speciosum*.

Opposite, left: *Dudleya pulverulenta*; right: *D. brittonii*.

DUDLEYA

Crassulaceae

These plants, native to the south-western United States and western Mexico, have rosettes that resemble some echeverias, and the upright facing leaves are covered in a white bloom or meal, which gives the rosette a silvery appearance. Their growth period is in late winter and spring, and they don't like wet conditions in their summer dormancy. Propagation is from seed, but is slow, and also from offsets if available; cuttings from old plants grow best in winter.

Dudleya brittonii

From Mexican arid tropical areas, this handsome plant has glaucous silver-grey leaves in a compact rosette. The leaves are red tipped later and then bluish, and the flowers are pale yellow.

Dudleya pulverulenta

The chalk lettuce, from southern California, has a very large rosette of silver-grey leaves, the plant forming a trunk with age. It bears small red flowers.

Dudleya traskiae

Also from southern California, this dudleya is a clustering form with small silver glaucous leaves.

DYCKIA

Bromeliaceae

This genus is made up of spiny-leaved rosette-forming evergreen perennials, from the tropical and subtropical regions of Brazil, Paraguay and Argentina. Infloresences are usually held above the foliage and the flowers are a tubular shape. They prefer full sun and good drainage, and are frost tender, standing a minimum of 5–7°C. Propagation from offsets or by division, best done in spring or summer.

Dyckia brevifolia

From South Brazil, and commonly called the miniature agave, this plant has a dwarf clustering rosette of deep green succulent sharp pointed leaves, with silver lines on the underside. The inflorescence is tall with numerous tubular yellow flowers.

Dyckia mariner-lopostollei

Heavily toothed and furrowed recurving silver-grey leaves over a dark red base make for a most interesting plant.

Dyckia platyphylla

This species has dark bronze-red leaves heavily armed with teeth and spines, and small tubular bright orange flowers on long stems.

Dyckia velascana

This plant has a pineapple-like foliage base of tapered leaves with light green teeth, which produces a branching inflorescence of yellow flowers. It is one of the largest species, the base an effective rosette of tapering foliage.

Left: *Dyckia velascana.*

ECHEVERIA

Crassulaceae

Although not the largest plants in the Crassulaceae family, echeverias are some of the most colourful, and their superior growth forms are spectacular. A number of them are under 15 cm in diameter, but some can reach up to 45 cm in width at the peak of their growth, which is when they flower, although after flowering there is usually a reduction in size.

Echeverias come from Mexico and surrounding countries and have become some of the most popular and sought after of the succulents.

Thick succulent leaves in rosette formations typify echeverias, and the surface of these can be waxy, hairy or covered in a white bloom or meal. The mature leaves are easily knocked off so care is necessary when handling them. Leaf colours range through white, grey, blue, green, pink, mauve, orange, red and brown with many fascinating shades in between that are difficult to describe; there are interesting seasonal changes in shades as well.

The bell-shaped flowers, many to each stem, are bright and attractive, in shades of yellow, orange, red and pink, and held as an inflorescence which usually arches at the top. They are long lasting on the plant and good for cut flowers.

While still retaining the typical rosette formation of leaves, a few species are branching plants and these are among the hardiest. *Echeveria multicaulis* is one of the branching species. In the non-branching forms, *E. elegans*, *E. secunda* and *E. imbricata* are fairly tolerant of wet and cold.

All echeverias can stand very cold temperatures if the potting mix or ground is dry and there is no moisture on the leaves, but they don't like constant rain on their leaves with cold conditions and this causes rot to develop and leaf drop. As for other

Above, left to right: *Echeveria* 'Topsy Turvy', *E. chiloense*, *E.* 'Giant Mexico', *E.* 'Mexico'.

succulents, the soil mix should be free draining.

They are attractive in glasshouse collections and often used as container plants or in sheltered spots outdoors, and massed plantings are very eye-catching. Areas where morning sunlight reaches the plants with afternoon shade to follow seem to bring out the texture and colouring of the leaves.

Many of the popular wavy- or curly-leaved echeverias are hybrids within the genus and their correct name can sometimes be difficult to ascertain, as nurseries tend to give plants their choice of name, which leads to different names for the same plant.

Echeverias have been crossed with other members of the Crassulaceae family, such as *Pachyphytum* and *Graptopetalum*, to produce plants with names such as *Pachyveria* and *Graptoveria*.

Propagation is from seed, leaves, offshoots, cuttings and flower stalks — methods can vary for different species. As often happens in the plant world, the most sought after varieties are the hardest to propagate.

Echeveria 'After Glow'

This is a very large cultivar, the leaves reaching about 16 cm long, and changing from a narrow pointed leaf at times to a very rounded and incurved shape at other times. The leaf colouring is strong with tones of pink, mauve and grey edged in red. The red bell-shaped flowers open on the arched ends of the trio of branches which gradually lengthen; there are usually three flowers out at a time on each branch, and each branch will have a total of around 25–30 flowers over the summer flowering period.

Top: *Echeveria* 'After Glow' flowers; left: *E.* 'After Glow'.

Echeveria agavoides

This has a large number of narrow, about 1 cm wide by 4 cm long, fleshy light green leaves tapering to a point, often red in colour. This form produces more offsets than the others.

Echeveria agavoides corderoyi

Has broader and more pointed deep green leaves, which colour deep red at the points in bright conditions. Sometimes these plants are given names like "lipstick", but often the difference between a brightly coloured plant and one with little red is the amount of light where they're grown. Only a few offsets are produced by this form.

Echeveria albicans

This species has rosettes 8–10 cm across, with thick glaucous blue leaves; fewer leaves and slightly darker in colour than the similar *E. elegans*. Flowers are pink at the base merging to yellow at the apex.

Echeveria 'Alfred Graffe'

Shiny tan-coloured broad leaves tapering to a point, with bright green in the centre of the new crown, make this echeveria unique.

Echeveria 'Alma Wilson'

This 35 cm diameter plant has firm waved and heavily frilled mid-green leaves, the edges turning light red with age.

Echeveria amoena

The rosettes of this plant are small and branches form from the base. It has short thick blue-grey leaves with rounded pinkish ends.

Top: *Echeveria* 'Alma Wilson'; right: *E. agavoides corderoyi* grown in sun (left) and shade (right).

Top left: *Echeveria* 'Crinoline'; top right: *E*. 'Blue Crinkles'; above left: *E*. 'Cinderella'; above right: *E*. 'Blue Butterfly'.

Echeveria 'Berkeley'

This plant has a large rosette of broad bluish leaves with reddish wavy edges.

Echeveria 'Black Prince'

One of the darkest coloured echeverias when grown in bright light, this hybrid has rosettes up to 18 cm wide. It has pointed narrowish leaves, 3 cm at the widest part and 6–8 cm long. Many inflorescences growing to about 40 cm high, and branched at the top, carry small red flowers in late autumn. Easily propagated from leaves.

Echeveria 'Blue Butterfly'

An attractive blue with delicate waved and frilled pink margins.

Echeveria 'Blue Crinkles'

A medium-size echeveria, it has blue-green leaves with pink frilled edges.

Echeveria 'Blue Waves'

Medium-sized, 15–18 cm wide, with blue leaves frilled in reddish pink. Rather shy at forming offsets.

Echeveria 'Brown Sugar'

This plant has a rosette 16–18 cm wide, with interesting deep brown, long tapering leaves with a red reverse.

Echeveria chiloense

This plant has broad blue leaves with lightly waved pink edges. The central new leaves are slightly incurved; leaves develop more pink as they mature.

Echeveria 'Cinderella'

A very large echeveria reaching up to 45–50 cm wide when mature. The leaves are green with red frilly edges, the whole leaves turn red as they age. Very long inflorescences produce reddish pink flowers on the branches.

Echeveria coccinea

A branching species with lightly furrowed green leaves covered in very fine hairs. The leaves are narrow at the base of the rosettes, widening three-quarters of the way along then tapering to a terminal point.

Echeveria 'Crest'

A tightly bunching form of bright green crowns with a little red colouring on the leaf tips.

Echeveria 'Crinoline'

Another very large cultivar, very similar to 'Cinderella'.

Above: *Echeveria* 'Black Prince'; left: *E. coccinea*.

Echeveria derex

These plants reach 20 cm in diameter, with bold rosettes of thick upward curving leaves 8 cm long by 5 cm wide; leaves are pinkish grey. Occasional offsets are produced.

Echeveria domingo

Has an attractive formal very pale grey rosette up to 22 cm wide, with a hint of pink in the older leaves that grow to 8 cm by 5 cm. Light salmon-coloured flowers are borne on branches at the top of a 40 cm stem.

Above: *Echeveria derex*; left: *E. domingo*.

Echeveria 'Doris Taylor'

The leaves on this plant are slightly incurving in the rosette, 4–5 cm long and 2 cm wide; they are basically green with a tiny bit of red on the tip, but have a silvery appearance due to the dense covering of white hairs. Stems about 15 cm long produce very bright orange and yellow flowers.

Echeveria 'Double Delight'

The features of this large hybrid are the greenish to pink leaves with wavy edges.

Right and below: *Echeveria* 'Doris Taylor'.

Top: *Echeveria elegans* (left), *E. albicans* (right);
above: *E.* 'Easter Bonnet'.

Echeveria 'Easter Bonnet'

The fluted leaves are a little narrower than most hybrids, and are pink over the blue-green leaf base.

Echeveria elegans

One of the most useful echeverias in the garden as it is clump forming, and will quickly spread completely over an area if desired. The pale blue-grey leaves are thick, rounded with a small terminal point, and packed in the rosette tightly; when stressed an attractive pink colouring is formed in some of the older leaves. Numerous pink stems about 30 cm high produce pink and yellow flowers.

Echeveria fasciculata

A large plant, it grows quite tall and reaches to 30 cm wide with a thick stem to 50 cm long after several years. The few leaves are smooth, slightly channeled, and dark green to red in colouring.

Echeveria fredissima

This plant has light green leaves with a narrow red margin arranged in a small rosette.

Echeveria 'Giant Mexico'

With its pointed cylindrical almost white leaves, this distinctive cultivar is an exciting plant to have among broad rounded-leaved echeverias. Plants can be 20–25 cm in diameter and will put out offsets from the base when they are doing well. Because the leaves are covered in a thick white bloom, rain and overhead watering tends to mark them a little. Propagation from offsets that grow around the base of the plant.

Right: *Echeveria fasciculata*; below: *E.* 'Giant Mexico'.

Echeveria gibbiflora metallica

The rosettes on this attractive plant reach about 22 cm diameter. It has broadly rounded leaves in a metallic purple-pink shade with smooth pink margins, and bright reddish pink flowerbuds produce long-lasting flowers. Plant in a dry well-sheltered position. Flower stems sometimes produce new plantlets.

Echeveria 'Gingerbread'

A large grower reaching 30–40 cm diameter, with dark purplish green wavy-edged leaves.

Echeveria ginmettenyo

Rosettes on this plant reach about 24 cm, and its light green colouring is an attractive foil set among other grey, pink or purple echeverias. The light green rounded leaves are edged with red, more colour spreading through the leaf as it matures. Occasionally a branch will develop, plantlets are often formed on the stems.

Echeveria 'Golden Glow'

This plant grows to about 25 cm in diameter, and has thick upward curving light green leaves with yellowish edges that colour more as they age.

Echeveria 'Golden State'

Variegations seem to be few among the echeverias, but this branching plant has streaks of pink, green and white mingling on rounded leaves.

Top: *Echeveria gibbiflora metallica*; left: *E. ginmettenyo*.

Echeveria 'Green Rose'

Small light green rosettes, branching with slightly reddish older leaves, gives this succulent the appearance of an old-fashioned green rose.

Echeveria 'Holly Gate'

A pale grey formal succulent, the tiered leaves widening outwards to form a small pink point at the apex. It reaches 15–20 cm in width.

Right: *Echeveria* 'Golden Glow'; below: *E.* 'Holly Gate'.

Echeveria imbricata

This is one of the hardiest forms available, and rosettes can reach 24 cm diameter in good conditions. It has a basic blue-grey colouring, but older leaves can turn quite bright pink. The abundant pink flowers with yellow linings to the petals make a good display.

Echeveria katella

There are several forms of E. katella, 'Princess' with shiny dark green leaves and frilly red edges, while others are numbered forms. E. katella IV has light green-blue leaves with pink edges.

This page, top left: Echeveria imbricata flowers; above: E. katella 'Princess'; left: E. katella IV.

Opposite, top: Echeveria imbricata; bottom: E. imbricata and E. chiloense (right).

Echeveria lilacina

The rosette on this echeveria can be 20 cm in diameter, with leaves up to 6 cm long and 4 cm wide. It is made up of formally placed very light blue-grey, almost spoon-shaped leaves with a small point at the tip of each one.

Echeveria lyndsayana

Thick leaves of very light blue-green with pink pointed tips are arranged in a rosette that grows to about 14 cm.

Echeveria 'Manda's Hybrid'

A strong growing medium-sized rosette with pale blue-grey leaves.

Echeveria 'Mauna Loa'

A very large grower reaching 30–40 cm, with blue-green leaves and deep reddish pink frilled edges, it is often seen in indoor collections. Sometimes older plants develop carunculation on the leaves.

This page, top left: *Echeveria lyndsayana*; top right and above: *E.* 'Mauna Loa' in different seasons of growth.

Opposite: *Echeveria lilacina*.

Echeveria 'Mexico City'

This strong-growing echeveria has very large light pink smooth leaves, sometimes with a hint of greenish grey, the plant reaching a diameter of 40 cm.

Echeveria multicaulis

A branching plant with rosettes of smallish deep green leaves, sometimes with dark red edges when conditions are very hot and dry. Bright red flowers with yellow interiors appear in winter. Excellent for mass planting in a suitable climate.

Echeveria pallida

This plant, with its rosette of about 25 cm, stands out in a collection of echeverias with its very light green colour and smooth rounded leaves.

Echeveria 'Party Dress'

Another of the large, pretty blue-green-leaved cultivars with frilly pink edges.

This page, top left: *Echeveria multicaulis* flowers; above: *E. pallida*; left: *E. multicaulis*.

Opposite, top: *Echeveria* 'Paul Bunyon'; bottom: *E.* 'Perle von Nurnberg'.

Echeveria 'Paul Bunyon'
(syn. *carunculata*)

This plant is interesting because of the overlayed thick knobbly growths or carunculation, which resemble another leaf on top of the normal leaves. The colouring is light purplish green, but in good light older leaves deepen to the metallic pink of *E. gibbiflora* from which it was propagated. Rosettes reach about 25 cm in width and height.

Echeveria 'Perle von Nurnberg'

This slow grower has rosettes up to 20 cm, made up of broad leaves with a tiny point at each tip in a glowing pink to purple colour. A hybrid from *E. potosina* x *E. gibbiflora metallica*.

Echeveria 'Pink Beauty'

Grown outdoors, this large 30 cm hybrid has open growth with light green leaves with a frilly reddish edge, but the overall effect is of light pink.

Echeveria 'Pink Marble'

A branching plant with quite heavy crowns of greyish pink leaves, almost semi-cylindrical in shape, which compliments other broader-leaved echeverias. Propagates freely from leaves and pieces.

Echeveria 'Powder Blue'

This cultivar has very light blue leaves with red edges, the red gradually extending down the leaf during summer. Propagate from offsets that appear freely.

Echeveria pulvinata

A branching plant with green leaves coated in fine white hairs and bright red ends.

Echeveria pulvinata ssp. Nova

Also branches like *E. pulvinata*, but has more white hairs and no red colouring.

Top left: *Echeveria* 'Pink Beauty'; above: *E.* 'Powder Blue'; bottom left: Flowers on *E. pulvinata* species; below: *E. pulvinata*.

Echeveria 'Rainbow'

This cultivar has light blue-green leaves with a red edge, the colours deepening as the leaves mature.

Echeveria 'Ruby Lips'

This plant grows to about 25 cm, and has large rounded leaves of deep blue green and a distinct red edge.

Echeveria runyoni

This species forms a small rosette to about 15 cm, made up of pale glaucous blue leaves, their outline rounded with a tiny terminal point from the centre of each leaf. It is a clustering plant, offsets forming around the base.

Echeveria runyoni glauca

Very similar to *E. runyoni* but more silvery grey in colour.

Top: *Echeveria* 'Rainbow'; above: *E.* 'Ruby Lips'.

Echeveria secunda

This has a blue-green clumping form, with the crowns slightly hollow in shape and the leaves coming to a definite point. This species is excellent for mass planting, and the red and yellow flowers add interest.

Echeveria shaviana

An attractive plant with its very frilly centre only reaches 14–16 cm wide. It has very thin grey leaves edged in white to light grey. Some plants produce many offsets.

Echeveria subrigida

This handsome plant usually reaches about 35 cm in diameter, although it is said that the leaves can be 25 cm long and 10 cm wide. It has a very formal rosette of very light silvery white leaves with red margins.

Echeveria subsellis

Formally tiered, the small light blue leaves edged with pink look very neat.

Echeveria 'Thelma O'Reilly'

An interesting plant with pointed dark brownish leaves with narrow white margins, and bearing orange flowers.

Echeveria 'Tina'

A small deep green rosette with red-edged leaves, a red keel on the reverse side and a very thin leaf tip.

Echeveria 'Topper'

Fluted leaves, a little narrower than most hybrids, filled pink over the blue-green leaf base.

Echeveria 'Topsy Turvy'

This cultivar of *E. runyoni* takes its name from the shape of the leaves, which reflex back down their length, giving the appearance of being upside down.

This page, top left: *Echeveria shaviana*; above: *E.* 'Topsy Turvy'; below: *E.* 'Topper'.

Opposite, top left: *Echeveria* 'Topsy Turvy' flowers; top right: *E. subsellis*; bottom: *E. secunda*.

Echeveria violescens

A smooth-edged species with thick pinkish mauve leaves.

Echeveria 'Violet Queen'

This cultivar is a smallish clumping grower with rosettes reaching 9–10 cm diameter. It has narrow very light blue-green leaves that turn pink as they age; the leaves tend to stand upright rather than reflexing and the offsets bunch around the sides. Its narrow leaves add a nice contrast when grown with other broad-leaved species.

Echeveria 'Yama'

This plant has a neat small blue-green rosette.

Echeveria 'Zorro'

A very large frilly dark purplish red plant reaching about 35 cm. The new central leaves are the only green on this plant.

Top left: *Echeveria* 'Violet Queen'; above: *E*. 'Zorro'.

EUPHORBIA

Euphorbiaceae

With over 300 genera and 8000 species in a 1990 listing, this is an enormous group of plants and one that combines all types. In fact few genera show as much variety as Euphorbia, which includes prostrate annual herbs to tall forest trees.

There are euphorbias of some kind native to every corner of the globe except Antarctica, although the majority come from tropical and subtropical areas. *Euphorbia obesa* from South Africa is a small tennis ball-sized leafless sphere and *E. ampliphylla* is an East African tree reaching 30 m high. Many euphorbias are very prickly, but there are also many herbaceous species like *E. characias* and *E. myrsinites* with the soft leaves typical of plants used widely in temperate gardens.

The most significant common feature to all euphorbias is the unusual flower structure. The flowers are much reduced, with no petals and no sepals, just modified coloured leaves designed to attract insects as pollinators. The second feature common to most euphorbias is the white poisonous sap, latex, which flows from any broken stem or wound on any part of the plant. Skin and eye problems can arise from this sap, so it is advisable to be protected when handling euphorbias. *E. virosa* is one of the worst for causing severe pain if brushed anywhere near the eyes; the juice of the succulent *Aeonium lindleyi* is recommended as an antidote.

The earliest written record of the medicinal use of euphorbias is associated with Hipprocates about 400 BC. The name *Euphorbia* is derived from Euphorbus, a physician to the King of Mauritania; other records state that euphorbias are supposed to have been discovered and named by King Juba II of Rome between 50 BC and AD 19. The name tithymalus

Below: *Euphorbia myrsinites.*

Above: *Euphorbia amygdaloides*.

Mediterranean area the green-flowered *E. characias*, now a well-known garden plant, was one of the species crushed and placed in a basket in a stream to poison fish. There are no reports on those who ate the fish!

Apparently the poison from *E. tirucalli* is still used in paint applied to the bottoms of boats to prevent marine organisms encrusting the boat.

An oil company has found that hydrocarbon for petrol can be extracted from crops of *E. lathyris* and a substantial amount of sugar as well as other substances can also be refined. The worry of soil erosion and the dangerous effect of the carcinogenic juice or sap of the euphorbia are perhaps holding up further work in this area.

Euphorbias have other uses too. *E. tirucalli* is used in India as a fast-growing thorny hedge, and grown as a 'milk hedge' between paddy fields in Sri Lanka. *E. hermentiana* used to be grown around settlements in the Congo as a lightning conductor.

In his book *Euphorbias*, Roger Turner notes that you can find amusement in euphorbia species' names: 'Euphorbias range from *enormis* to *miniata*, from *montrosa* to *liliputiana*, from *splendens* to *inelegans*, and from *magnificum* and *grandis* to *horrida* and *vulgaris*.

'They come in varying shades of *greenei*, *whitei*, *brownii*, and *purpurea*, and may be *cylindrical*, *triangularis*, *quadrangularis*, *quinqueradiata*, *sexangularis*, *septemsulcata* or even *octoradiata*.'

The thoughts of Gertrude Jekyll in her 1908 book *Colour Schemes for the Garden* are also worth noting: 'A wonderful plant of May is the great *Euphorbia wulfenii*. It adapts itself to many ways of use, for, though the immense yellow green heads are at their best in May, they are still of pictorial value in June

was given to Greek spurges, spurge being a common name for euphorbias as the seeds of the caper spurge were used as a purgative in the Middle Ages and the juice of all spurges were said to have been recommended as a 'laxatyve' and 'a strong medicine to open the bellie'. Catapus was the medieval Latin name of one of the spurges and the Italian version was an unpleasant sounding cacapuzza.

The powerful poisonous latex of *E. reinhardtii* in Sudan and *E. hermentiana* in tropical Africa were used on arrows to catch prey, and in Madagascar *E. primulifolia* was used as a rat poison. In the and July, while the deep toned grey blue foliage is in full beauty throughout the year.'

E. *peplus*, on the other hand, is that soft little milk weed that pops up in every garden, having flowered and dropped seeds before you realise it. This plant adapts to shade or full sun — any place will do! It has spread round the world from Europe, the Mediterranean and Siberia.

Propagation of euphorbias is easy from seed, many self sowing where the soil is warm. Most can be grown from cuttings and sometimes rooted basal pieces can be removed from the plant.

Euphorbia amygdaloides

This open woodland species from England and Europe is usually listed as a perennial, but in my temperate situation it often doesn't last more than 2 years. However, it is worth enjoying while there for its foliage and floral display as well as numerous seedlings. The new reddish purple foliage appears before the bright lime-green flowerheads, growing to 60 cm, and is attractive in the garden; the older deep blue-green leaves make a good background. Inflorescences appear in spring, and several main stems reaching about 15 cm in length arise from the base of the plant, these producing smaller branches. Semi-shade seems ideal for this species which is prone to mildew and thrips.

Euphorbia amygdaloides purpurea & rubra

These are both cultivars of E. *amygdaloides*, but it is very difficult to tell whether one is a cultivar or a natural variation of the species, as natural variation occurs in the wild and in cultivated seedlings with some darker than others.

Above: Euphorbia characias syn. E. wulfenii.

Euphorbia characias syn. E. wulfenii

This very strong evergreen perennial euphorbia comes from dry scrublands, rocky areas and open forests of the Mediterranean. It has many upright stems that can reach over 1 m high, with blue-green foliage; in its second year some of the stems flower with dense heads 15–20 cm in diameter which last about 2 months on the plant. Once the flowerheads start to brown off, it is advisable to cut their stems back close to the base taking care not to get the milk sap on skin or near eyes and keeping the poisonous prunings away from stock. If seed is required, some mature heads can be left to disperse seed, which will be flung about the plant, but if collection is necessary, a paper bag tied over the head will collect the seeds as they burst out. Each plant can last 8–10 years, so it is very worthwhile in the right situation; dry soils and full sun are preferred but it will grow in partial shade, although the stems elongate and there are less flowering heads if too much shade. It is recommended by botanists that E. *characias* and its subspecies E. *wulfenii* are both called E. *characias* as the two are so similar.

Euphorbia characias 'Burrow Silver'

This is an attractive variegated form, which has tall upright stems, up to 1 m high, clad in green leaves with yellow margins in the new growth and fading to cream as they age. Creamy yellow flowers with a green stripe make it stand out in the garden.

Euphorbia cornigera

A deciduous perennial from Pakistan and northern India, which reaches up to 1 m in height, with deep green long narrow leaves with a light central rib. The bright yellowish lime flowerhead is branched, flattish at the top with several side branches of flowers; flowers appear in summer. Good drainage is preferred, propagation from seed or division.

Euphorbia cyparissia 'Orange Man'

This looks attractive as a low-growing very fine-leaved plant with lime-yellow flowers that turn orange as they age. The fine leaves are almost like pine needles. Gardeners beware: this plant sends out far-reaching rhizomes, which very quickly form new plants so can be a dangerous spreader.

Above: *Euphorbia characias* 'Burrow Silver'; top right: *E. cornigera*; right: *E. cyparissia* 'Orange Man'.

Euphorbia decaryi

This is a collectors' plant, prostrate in form with thick stems, wavy-edged narrow green leaves in terminal clusters, and short-stemmed groups of fawn flowers.

Euphorbia echinus

One of the very thick-stemmed succulent leafless euphorbias with many spines and tiny red flowers. A plant for the hot dry bank.

Euphorbia grandicans

A branching succulent with many curving 3-angled stems of green, each edge adorned with fierce 2–5 cm long paired spines, brown at first but turning to grey as they age. A popular euphorbia for collectors.

Above: *Euphorbia decaryi*; top right: *E. echinus*; right: *E. grandicans*.

Euphorbia horrida

The common name for this species is African milk barrel. It has clustered crowns of amazing spines much like the true cacti.

Euphorbia ingens

From warm areas of South Africa such as Natal and Transvaal, this candelabra tree can reach 10 m high. The stems and branches are either 4 or 5 angled and the plant is completely leafless, but has minute flowers on the nodes which set seed. Propagation from seed or cuttings.

Euphorbia mammillaris

This is one of the succulents from Cape Province, South Africa, that sends up numerous erect branches to form a dense clump, sometimes up to 1 m in diameter in the wild. *E. submammillaris* is a tidy mounding pot plant to 20 cm high.

Euphorbia mellifera

This Canary Islands' native with bright green bushy growth is a shrub about 1.5 m high in the garden, although it is said to reach a tree-like 15 m in its natural habitat. Nobbly flowerheads rise above the bright green leaves with white midribs. In frost-free dry areas this plant is troubled only occasionally by thrips and spider mites. Seedlings come up freely in light sandy soil.

Top left: *Euphorbia horrida*; left: *E. ingens*.

Euphorbia milii

The common name of this sprawling plant from Madagascar is crown of thorns. It has prickly woody stems, small clusters of bright green deciduous leaves, and eyecatching bracts of minute red flowers. Needs a warm dry situation.

Euphorbia milii alba

An identical form to *E. milii*, but with cream flowers.

Euphorbia x martinii

This is a natural hybrid of *E. characias* and *E. amygdaloides*. A number of foliage stems rise from a single crown to about 70 cm high, the leaves are greyish green. The attractive massed head is made up of many small cupped lime-green flowers that turn bronze as they age for an autumn-coloured display. Cuttings are the only means of propagation.

Above: *Euphorbia submammillaris*; top right: *E. mellifera*; right: *E. milii*.

This page, top: *Euphorbia myrsinites*; above: *E. nicaeensis* 'Blue Peaks'; right: *E. obtusifolia* var. *regis jubae*.

Opposite, left: *Euphorbia schillingii*; right: *E. rigida*.

Euphorbia myrsinites

This species comes from a wide area of rocky and sandy places on the Mediterranean. Short pointed blue-grey leaves spiral around the stems and spread from the crown to about 40 cm wide. The terminal clusters of yellow-green flowers appear in spring; it is best to cut the spent stems back to the crown once flowering is finished, new growth will soon spring away again. This is a very popular euphorbia for rockeries and dry banks. Seed will set freely if the flowers are left long enough.

Euphorbia nicaeensis 'Blue Peaks'

The species *E. nicaeensis* is apparently variable over a wide area of the Mediterranean and was named around 1760. The bluish foliage is attractive in this form and the lime-yellow floral bracts are an interesting contrast in late summer. This plant prefers warm situations, and can be propagated from seed, although slight variations in colour may occur.

Euphorbia obtusifolia var. regis jubae

This many-branched shrub grows to about 1 m high, with rounded succulent light fawn stems showing indentations from old leaf bases. It has very narrow green leaves, and clusters of small floral parts top each of the branches.

Euphorbia rigida

Another very good Mediterranean species with beautiful pointed glaucous blue leaves on upcurving stems reaching 60 cm long. The floral leaves are lime yellow and aged flowers can turn orange. A handsome plant for dry areas away from extreme cold. Propagation from seed is preferable, as it is difficult from cuttings.

Euphorbia schillingii

This euphorbia comes from Nepal and was introduced by the man who discovered it, Tony Schilling. Unbranched stems reaching about 1 m high rise from the base, while deep green leaves with light midribs clothe part of the stems and lime-yellow flowers are held in flattish racemes above. The plant is reasonably hardy except in the coldest areas. Propagation from cuttings, seed or by division.

Euphorbia splendens

This euphorbia is similar to *E. milii*, but has larger leaves and floral bracts and is not as hardy.

Euphorbia stenoclada

This leafless many-branched prickly shrub from Madagascar grows to 2 m high, and is a beautiful silver colour. It can make a completely impenetrable thicket.

Euphorbia trigona

This is a strictly upright small tree from Namibia, with 3- or 4-angled stems. These stems are lightly patterned on the smooth inner areas, with the outer edges carrying pairs of thorns and sometimes 2 cm long leaves on them. The leaves can be green or red, depending on the form, and they appear on the upper sections when the plant is having a growth period. Minute flowers sometimes form on the upper ridges. An exciting and different collectors' plant suitable for a container or the warm dry garden.

Euphorbia woodii

A prostrate-growing plant with numerous stems radiating from the crown, and yellow flowers displayed around the central area. A useful low plant for the dry rockery.

Top left: *Euphorbia trigona*; above: *E. stenoclada*; left: *E. woodii*.

FAUCARIA

Aizoaceae

Faucaria come from Cape Province, South Africa, and Namibia. They are mostly stemless plants with thick 3-sided leaves, usually with downward pointing teeth. Large daisy-like yellow flowers appear in late summer. They need little water but can stand some moisture in summer, and are best in free-draining potting mix.

Faucaria longifolia

This species has light green leaves with downward pointing soft white teeth on the upper half and short stems showing under old clumps. Propagation from seed or cuttings.

Faucaria tuberculosa

Thick deep green tubercled leaves with a few soft teeth on the upper halves are typical of this species. Yellow flowers appear in late summer and autumn. Propagation from cuttings and seed.

Above: *Faucaria tuberculosa.*

FENESTRARIA

Aizoaceae

These small plants from the dry deserts of Namibia are commonly known as babies' toes. The name 'fenestraria' is derived from 'fenestra' meaning window and refers to the translucent top on each of the cylindrical leaves which allows light to enter the plant. Light is necessary for the plant to manufacture chlorophyll and in desert conditions where blown sand can restrict the light reaching small plants, the window on the upper surface allows enough light to be absorbed.

Quite large flowers for the size of the plants appear in late summer to autumn. Their growth period is in early summer when they can be given light watering, but they must have no water during winter and their potting mix must be very porous. They require full sunlight, and like *Lithops*, are best treated as indoor plants. Propagation from seed.

Fenestraria aurantiaca

This plant can form a clump up to 10 cm across, and bears club-shaped light green leaves with translucent tops. The bright yellow flowers bloom on a stem about 5 cm long.

Fenestraria rhopalophylla

This species also clumps to 10 cm, and has light grey-green leaves with translucent tops and white flowers.

Below: *Fenestraria aurantiaca.*

FICUS

Moraceae

The fig family is large and varied, and covers enormous trees, rubber plants, stranglers, banyans, even creepers and climbers, as well as some members which are xerophytic desert-climate trees with swollen bases.

Ficus palmerii

This is one of the desert-climate trees with a thickened base, and is from Baja California. In ideal conditions and with plenty of food and water, this plant can reach 4 m in less than 2 years. It is also interesting as an indoor collectors' plant for the basal form. Propagation from seed.

Above: *Ficus palmerii.*

Right: *Fockea edulis.*

FOCKEA

Asclepiadaceae

Fockeas, African xerophytic plants, are known for their caudex and are becoming popular as collectors' plants. They need well-drained conditions and little watering. Propagation is from seed.

Fockea edulis

This species bears climbing or trailing stems up to 80 cm long, with small green leaves, the stems growing from a thickened base that is sometimes bottle shaped. The base can reach 30 cm in diameter in a container, but old ones can reach huge proportions in their natural habitat. The edible fleshy base is said to be a substitute for melon.

FURCRAEA

Agavaceae

Furcraeas have undergone many name changes: *Roezlia*, *Agave*, *Yucca* and *Beschorneria* before *Furcraea* was deemed to be the correct or most suitable genus name.

Furcraeas grow naturally in deciduous tropical forests and open areas from Mexico to Brazil, and are very large rosette-shaped plants with sword-shaped leaves similar to agaves and yuccas. Some grow from ground level with no stem and others can reach 5–6 m on very tall stems more like trunks. The leaves are not as well armed with teeth as agaves, although some species do have small ones, nor do they have the sharp terminal spines.

These bold plants are suited to well-drained gardens in coastal areas of the temperate zones of the world. Propagation from bulbils or seed.

Furcraea bedinghausii

This species is often confused with the larger-growing *F. roezlii*, and has glaucous blue-green leaves just over 50 cm long by 5–7 cm wide on a trunk that seldom reaches 1 m.

Furcraea foetida

This species is grown commercially for fibre on Mauritius Island, hence its common name Mauritius hemp. It is usually a trunkless species although some plants have been known to have a small trunk. It produces offsets which will eventually form a clump. The green leaves have a rough underside and a few very small teeth on the lower edges, but have no spine; the leaves can reach over 2 m long in suitable conditions. The inflorescence reaches to 7.5 m and is loosely branched with perfumed greenish flowers.

Furcraea foetida var. medio-picta

This is a very good variegated form of *F. foetida*, which has been grown as an ornamental for many years. Growth patterns are similar to *F. foetida* although heavily variegated plants don't always grow quite as large as the green form. This plant makes a strong focal point as a single crown or as a clump.

Left: *Furcraea foetida* var. *medio-picta*.

Opposite, top: *Furcraea roezlii*; bottom: *F. roezlii* flowers.

Furcraea roezlii

Long broad blue-green strap-shaped leaves, up to 1 m long, form a very large rosette up to 2 m wide in this species. Growth starts from ground level and after 2–3 years the stem becomes obvious as the rosette rises. The leaves are rough on the edges and undersides and the margins are lined with minute teeth; the older leaves hang down against the stem or trunk as it lengthens. The plant eventually flowers (mine took about 12 years), but conditions no doubt govern this, and the inflorescence reaches 3–5 m above the crown of the rosette. The inflorescence branches, forming a huge pyramidal shape of clusters of light green pendent flowers, which form seed pods as they mature; the branches also form hundreds of bulbils, ready to grow as soon as they fall off. This plant will stand light frosts but is not recommended for areas with severe cold. Propagates readily from offsets.

Furcraea selloa marginata

This is a popular ornamental form in frost-free areas. The trunk can reach 1.5 m with a rosette of stiff leaves on top, and clustered offsets can appear around the base. The leaves, up to 1.2 m long, have small hooked brown teeth on the margins; and cream to yellow streaks also appear along the margins and sometimes elsewhere on the 8 cm wide leaves. A large inflorescence up to 6 m long bears greenish flowers and many bulbils are formed as the flowers fade. This plant grows in full sun, except in desert conditions where shade is important, it can also tolerate semi-shade. Propagation from offsets.

GASTERIA

Liliaceae

Gasterias are low slow-growing green succulents from South Africa with stiff thick leaves. The leaves on many gasterias grow in two ranks, stacked evenly on top of each other. Other species grow their leaves in a star-shaped rosette but most have small dots or tubercles on the leaf surfaces.

The attractive inflorescences have a tall stem, sometimes branched, densely covered in waxy globular salmon-pink flowers with a narrower greenish tubular opening.

They prefer a dry warm climate and semi-shade, often adding to collections of succulents housed by enthusiasts. Propagate from leaf cuttings and offshoots.

Above: *Gasteria armstrongii*; right: *G. brachyphylla*.

Gasteria armstrongii

Tiered thick dark green leaves, about 10 cm long, which reflex strongly are typical of this species.

Gasteria brachyphylla

A stemless plant that reaches 25 cm high, with many small white tubercles on the leaves.

Gasteria croucheri

A strong-growing species with green speckled leaves, wide at the base and strongly tapering at the tips.

Gasteria liliputana

This species grows in a cluster of stemless crowns, light coloured spotty variegations in the narrow green leaves.

Gasteria neliana

This plant has dark green stiff leaves heavily spotted with tubercles, and will produce offsets.

Top right: *Gasteria neliana*; right: *G. croucheri*; below: *G. liliputana*.

Gasteria nigricans

This is one of the larger-growing species with variegation in the leaves, which tolerates full sun in a temperate climate when most gasterias prefer semi-shade. The graceful waxy globular salmon pink flowers are freely produced in warm conditions.

Gasteria rostii

This is a light green species with a few dark green streaks on the leaves.

This page, right: *Gasteria rostii*; below: G. *nigricans* in flower.

Opposite, top left: *Gasteria tegeliana*; top right: G. *verrucosa*; bottom: G. *variegata*.

Gasteria tegeliana

One of the species that has a star-shaped rosette, very stiff leaves, green to bronze as they age and heavily tubercled.

Gasteria variegata

This plant bears an occasional light yellow streak.

Gasteria verrucosa

This plant has many small raised tubercles, and tends to be grown outdoors more than other gasterias.

GASWORTHIA

Liliaceae

Attractive hybrids between Gasteria and Haworthia are called gasworthias and appear to show some of the best features of the two genera.

Gasworthia 'Banded Pearls'

A dark green rosette of longish pointed leaves with very white tubercles on all surfaces is typical of this plant.

Gasworthia tegeliana

Stiff dark green leaves speckled with numerous white tubercles make this an attractive plant.

Right: *Gasworthia tegeliana*; below: G. 'Banded Pearls'.

GRAPTOPETALUM

Crassulaceae

Graptopetalum are from Mexico and bear rosettes of thick leaves, the plants branching ultimately with more terminal crowns, all of which resemble echeverias, with which they are said to hybridise.

They grow in full sun but can stand partial shade as long as the conditions are warm and dry rather than wet. They are very useful container and rockery plants and are easily propagated from leaves or stems.

Graptopetalum pachyphytoides

This branching plant has thick oval pointed blue-grey leaves which age to reddish and yellow shades. Propagate from crowns or leaves.

Graptopetalum paraguayense

Sometimes called a ghost plant, this species is from Mexico, a branching succulent with loose rosettes of thick flat leaves of silvery grey, sometimes flushed with pink, with a surface bloom. These leaves knock off easily, but if left in a warm dry place will grow a baby plant from the end. Sprays of white flowers appear on this plant which needs warm dry conditions.

Above: *Graptopetalum paraguayense.*

GRAPTOVERIA

Crassulaceae

Graptoverias, as the name suggests, are crosses between Graptopetalum and Echeveria and grow in similar conditions.

Graptoveria 'Silver Star'

Small plants always attract attention with their neat appearance. They have very compact stemless rosettes of shiny silver-green leaves with long thin pink tips that look like thin spines, but are soft. Propagate from offsets.

Below: *Haworthia allasonii.*

HAWORTHIA

Liliaceae

These fascinating little plants are from Cape Province, South Africa, and Namibia and some species have windowed leaves where translucent areas allow light into the body of the plant to form chlorophyll. Other species have tubercles similar to gasterias, a closely related genus and there are some hybrids between the two.

The leaf margins bear teeth in some species and while many are stemless, others are stemmed and the leaves can reach 20 cm high, so it is a very variable genus. The flowers, on top of long stems, are mostly white with the 6 petals opening from a tubular base.

Haworthias prefer semi-shade, to be watered well in summer and kept dry in winter. They group well with gasterias, which like the same conditions. Propagation from offsets and seed.

Haworthia allasonii

This species has very thick leaves tightly set in rosettes, and the keeled leaves are translucent with a few dark green streaks over a light green base on the upper surfaces.

Haworthia attenuata

Narrow spiky leaves with bands of white tubercles give the outside of the leaves a zebra-patterned look. The plant is reasonably hardy in a temperate climate and multiplies freely from the base.

Haworthia attenuata var.

This is an interesting form of *H. attenuata* with bold cream streaks on the leaves.

Haworthia cymbiformis

Rosettes of translucent light green leaves with darker streaks can grow to about 10 cm diameter. Propagation from offsets.

Top: *Haworthia attenuata*; above: *H. cymbiformis*.

Haworthia emelyae

This species has leaves that would be hard to see in natural habitat as they are recurved and flattened to a triangle in the upper third of the leaf, so lie parallel with the ground. A dark green base with mid-green stripes and light green tubercles over the upper surface creates a fascinating design, laid out to allow just the right amount of light into the plant.

Haworthia hobdomadis morrisiae

A tight rosette of very fleshy thick pointed leaves streaked with light and dark green.

Haworthia limifolia

The fascinating texture of this small plant from Transvaal, South Africa, shows up more when wet. The pointed dark green leaves are stiff in the 8 cm rosette, and an inflorescence reaching 30 cm produces small white flowers.

Haworthia retusa

This plant from Cape Province, South Africa, has light green thick leaves, reflexed in the upper third, with dark green stripes on the upper surface. Many offsets cluster round the plant, which can be reddish coloured in bright outdoor conditions in its natural habitat.

Haworthia truncata

The unusual truncated or flat-topped leaves of this small plant have their windows across the top, and the surface has interesting patterns and very small tubercles. The inflorescence forms on a very tall 30–40 cm high stem which carries small white flowers. A fun plant for any collection.

Haworthia truncata magnifica

A similar plant to *H. truncata* but the growth and arrangement of the windowed leaves is mounding.

This page, top right: *Haworthia retusa*; right: *H. truncata magnifica*; below: *H. truncata*.

Opposite, top left: *Haworthia emelyae*; top right: *H. limifolia*; bottom: *H. hobdomadis morrisiae*.

Haworthia venosa var. tesselata

This species has small rosettes 8–10 cm wide, of deep green leaves with light grey-green lines forming a 'crazy paving' pattern. Very small light-coloured teeth are present on the leaf margins and small tubercles are spread over the undersides. Like most of this family, the inflorescence rises on a tall stem 40–50 cm high.

Haworthia uniondalensis

Glossy triangular leaf tips with linear patterns on very dark reddish green leaf bases make this plant hard to find among dark pebbles. A fine specimen and one most collectors would appreciate and treasure.

Top: *Haworthia venosa* var. *tesselata*;
above: *H. uniondalensis*.

HECHTIA

Bromeliaceae

Hechtias are hardy plants with curving prickly edged leaves radiating from the crown. They are related to dyckias but their flowers are not as interesting; however, the foliage is very worthwhile as a landscaping plant. Propagation from seed or offsets.

Hechtia argentea

This is considered one of the best species and its silver foliage makes a noteworthy statement in the garden. It shows the clumping habit of some bromeliads but is very much more hardy and prickly. An ideal plant for foliage colour in the dry garden.

Above: *Hechtia argentea.*

HOYA

Asclepiadaceae

Most hoyas are climbing plants from tropical regions, succulence appearing in their thick leaves. There are many cultivars available with clusters of beautiful small flowers, but all need warm conditions. Propagation from seed and, with difficulty, from cuttings.

Hoya carnosa

Commonly called the wax plant, this species is from India, Burma and south China, and has thick fleshy yet firm glossy green leaves. The beautiful flowers that form in pendent umbels are fragrant, and have to be admired close up for the velvety texture of the bracts and the waxiness of the central petals with their deep-coloured centres. These plants are often grown indoors but can be successfully grown in sheltered shadehouses in temperate climates.

Hoya pubicalyx 'Red Buttons'

A beautiful cultivar, the small shiny deep red flowers are set tightly against velvet-covered bracts.

Top: *Hoya pubicalyx* 'Red Buttons'; above: *H. carnosa*.

JOVIBARBA

Crassulaceae

This genus, from the Alps of Italy and France, is very closely allied to Sempervivum. They are prolific clustering little plants, each crown measuring only 2–3 cm but they send out many babies, sometimes called rollers; some species can differ in that offsets are tightly joined at the base. Close examination of the flowers identifies jovibarbas with a fimbriated petal edge not seen in sempervivums.

Propagation is easy from the baby rollers set on top of the soil, but in the tight growing forms divisions have to be carefully cut away.

Jovibarba allionii

This is the most commonly grown species with light green leaves that turn quite red at times. It is a clustering plant with many babies pushed upwards and outwards; each crown measures only 2–3 cm. The greenish white flowers are held in a group on a stem above the plant.

Above and below: *Jovibarba allionii.*

KALANCHOE

Crassulaceae

Most of the kalanchoes in cultivation come from
Africa and Madagascar but further species are native
to India, China, Malaya and other tropical regions.
They are generally not large plants, although
Kalanchoe beharense can reach about 3 m high.

In some cases different species are easily identified
by their foliage as they show one or more specific
characteristics. Some are completely smooth while
some bear a dense covering of hairs, some have
scalloped and toothed leaf margins, while others
produce numerous plantlets on the edges; foliage
colours range from silver, greys, greens, glaucous
blue, pink to red, and can also be flecked or
variegated.

The flowers have 4 petals, several species are
yellow, while others are lavender, pink, red, white
and orange.

As a rule kalanchoes don't like frost and some of
them must have dry conditions, particularly the
felted leaf types; others need warm, moist conditions
for their succulent growth.

Kalanchoe beharense

One of the special kalanchoes, this can reach 3 m
high, with huge 30 cm arrow-shaped leaves heavily
felted on both sides. The leaves on young plants are
greenish grey but as they mature in hot dry
conditions the colour changes to a rusty brown with
some grey. The woody trunks on older specimens are
unusually marked by deep depressions where older
leaves have fallen off. There are some cultivated
forms of this species which have horny prot-
uberances under the leaves. Propagation from leaf
stems and bases.

Kalanchoe blossfeldiana

This species from Madagascar is a compact branching plant reaching about 30 cm high, with bright shiny green leaves that sometimes turn red. Showy red flowers grow in clusters above the foliage, making this a desirable house-plant with several cultivars available in other colours. Propagation from basal pieces and cuttings.

Kalanchoe daigremontiana

This strong-growing plant has masses of plantlets along the leaf margins. The soft fleshy leaves are red edged, notched and flecked with purple on the reverse. Propagation from plantlets that root once reaching the soil.

Kalanchoe fedtschenkoi

An attractive and tidy garden plant throughout the year, with the pink flowers adding extra colour in spring. The notched pink-edged blue-grey leaves are held almost vertical on branches about 45 cm long. Propagation from cuttings.

This page, above: *Kalanchoe blossfeldiana*; top right: *K. fedtschenkoi*; right: *K. daigremontiana*.

Opposite: *Kalanchoe beharense*.

Kalanchoe grandiflora

This species, when mass planted, makes a useful blue-grey mass of foliage about 50 cm high. The loose clusters of yellow flowers on mature plants tend to fall over. Valuable as a groundcover in sunny or dry partially shaded areas such as under trees. This species is easily propagated from cuttings, preferably with the cut stem end dried before planting.

Kalanchoe grandiflora variegated

Has a similar form to K. *grandiflora* but needs pinching back to force new growth and a good variegated display.

Kalanchoe longiflora var. coccinea

This is spectacular as an upright rockery plant, reaching about 45 cm high, especially when the thick reddish leaves develop an intense red colouring. The leaves are heavily serrated or scalloped and the yellow flowers are small and produced on a thin stem. Propagates easily from cuttings.

This page, above and left: *Kalanchoe grandiflora*.

Opposite, top: *Kalanchoe pubescens*; bottom left: *K. longiflora* var. *coccinea*; bottom right: *K. marmorata*.

Kalanchoe marmorata

Sometimes called the penwiper plant. A strong
species with bold broad fleshy leaves, which are
bluish green when young and later flecked with dark
purple blotches. Evenly-spaced shallow notches
show clearly on leaf margins and the flowers are
white. Propagation from cuttings.

Kalanchoe pubescens

This strong-growing plant reaches 1 m high and
makes a good background plant for poor dry soil
areas. It has roundish hairy leaves that are green
when young and soft, and the pendent orange
flowers are held in clusters on thin stems. Numerous
plantlets form around the flowerhead, and once
flowering is finished these drop off, spreading the
plant naturally.

Kalanchoe pumila

This is a tidy dwarf grower with many uses, not only for containers and small spaces, but also as an effective and compact silver plant in a group. The attractive silver-grey leaves are notched on the outer edges, and in full sun they develop a reddish purple colouring. The mauve-pink 4-petalled flowers are a colourful bonus when in bloom. Take care when handling the plant, as the dusty bloom covering the whole leaf surface is easily rubbed off. Propagation from cuttings or basal pieces.

Kalanchoe synsepala

Known as the cup kalanchoe due to its leaf shape, this has an unusual growth habit, the crowns sitting on the ground and their offspring growing away from the plant on thin apron strings. It has 6–8 large curved light green leaves with an inner red margin and then an irregular margin of yellowish teeth.

To propagate, simply cut the ties from the parent plant and move the new plant away.

Kalanchoe thyrsiflora 'Bronze Sculpture'

An exciting plant with its large 15 cm round leaves which can be either flat or elegantly curved. The glaucous blue-green leaves have red edges of varying widths, depending on conditions, and as the plant elongates to flower, the leaves show a silver bloom which lights up the plant further. The flowers are yellow and after flowering new growths come away at the plant base. Basal divisions can be carefully removed for propagation.

This page: *Kalanchoe pumila*.

Opposite, top left and right: *Kalanchoe thyrsiflora* 'Bronze Sculpture'(right shows more advanced growth); bottom left: *K. synsepala*; bottom right: *K. tomentosa*.

Kalanchoe tomentosa

An upright grower to 35 cm high, with thick hairy brown-tipped, silver-grey leaves. It needs dry conditions and is not suited to outdoor planting in high rainfall areas, but is very useful in containers in dry places. Propagates easily from aerial roots and leaf bases.

Above and top right: *Kalanchoe tubiflora.*

Kalanchoe tubiflora

A slim little plant that can grow up to 60 cm high, with many plantlets on the end of each leaf. Pinkish leaves are almost cylindrical and heavily speckled with brown. The plantlets drop off and multiply almost to weed proportions, but they are a wonderful plant for children to nurture. The flowers are an amazing size, up to 3 cm long, in comparison with the slim little plant.

LAMPRANTHUS

Aizoaceae

Often called Mesembryanthemums, or ice plants, these South African plants are spectacular during their short flowering season and the foliage is pleasing as either a trailing groundcover or low bushy perennial. They are useful for dry sandy areas, rockeries and banks. Propagation from cuttings.

Lampranthus aureum

This species has masses of shiny orange flowers and narrow fleshy green leaves.

Lampranthus blandus

Shiny daisy-like bright pink flowers with clustered white stamens in the centre are produced terminally above narrow fleshy green leaves on a bushy plant. Prune after flowering for compact plants and use the cuttings for propagation.

Top left: *Lampranthus aureum*; above: *L. deltoides* syn. *Oscularia deltoids*.

Lampranthus deltoides
syn. Oscularia deltoides

This plant is interesting for its knobbly short thick blue-green foliage with small red teeth and red stems. Flowers are pink.

Above: *Lampranthus multiradiatus*; top right: *L.* species as groundcover; below: *L. spectabilis*.

Lampranthus multiradiatus

This species has fine green foliage and pink flowers.

Lampranthus spectabilis

A bushy plant, reaching about 40 cm high, with bright cyclamen-pink flowers.

LITHOPS

Aizoaceae

Lithops are perhaps the most popular of the living stones type succulents and are easy to grow providing one or two basic requirements are strictly observed. They come from Namibia, and Cape Province and Transvaal in South Africa, and will be bigger when grown in cultivation than their natural habitat allows.

The many patterns and colours of their leaf surfaces are fascinating as they mimic the gravel or stone of the native habitat where they're tucked unobtrusively into cracks and corners of rock and sand for survival. The first instructions I had regarding the watering of lithops stated that if they had too much water they would get bloated and burst! A terrible thought but that is exactly what happens; although not a dramatic explosion or mess, they will quietly split, spoiling the appearance of those leaves.

Each year plants grow a new pair of leaves set in the opposite direction to the previous two and the old ones wither away. Lithops flower in autumn on sunny days with shining bright yellow or white stemless flowers appearing between the leaves.

It is preferable that lithops be grown in containers so that growing conditions can be controlled. The potting mix recommended is very free draining: a little loam, coarse sand, pumice grit, gravel, leaf mould and about a quarter of coarser material such as broken limestone or crushed brick. This should last them for 2 years. Water only on warm days between late spring and early autumn (the warm months) and not at all during winter. Use deep pots as they have long roots, and place on the brightest window ledges that get sun most of the day. A layer of fine gravel on the top of the containers helps keep the leaf surfaces dry.

Lithops can be propagated from seed with moisture, warmth and shade, and gradual introduction to drier conditions. Division of clumps can result in losses.

Top: *Lithops* flowers; above: *L. lesliei* ssp. *lesliei* var. *rubrobrunnea.*

Lithops bronfieldii var. *menellii*
Known for its deeply-set brown patterns.

Lithops dorotheae
This has a greyish body with dark brown markings.

Lithops hallii
Has a grey body with small raised grey dots intermingled with dark brown dots.

Lithops karasmontana ssp. *Bellas*
These plants have greyish bodies with bold green-brown markings.

Lithops lesliei var. *albinica*
Has a green leaf body with fine darker green patterns.

Lithops lesliei ssp. *lesliei* var. *rubrobrunnea*
This plant has light tan leaves with dark brown and tan markings.

Lithops lesliei var. *venteri*
A greyish plant with fine dark greenish markings.

Lithops localis
A light brown-grey body has fine dark spots over a tan upper surface.

Lithops optica rubra
This plant has reddish leaves and translucent windows with little pattern.

Lithops otzeniana
Has half-moon shaped, darkish grey-green translucent leaf tops with light grey markings like teeth.

Lithops vallis-mariae
A variable species with fine dark patterns on light grey.

Lithops aucampiae
This species has fine brown patterns on large grey to fawn leaves.

Lithops culmanni
This plant has a smooth upper surface with fine tan dots.

Top: *Lithops localis*; above: *L. optica rubra*.

MANFREDA

Agavaceae

These rosette-forming plants from Mexico and the eastern states of the United States, with long narrow soft fleshy concave leaves, rather like an elongated aloe, bear very tall inflorescences with small flowers that open at night and have perfume.

Propagation can be from seed, the plants taking 3 years to bloom, or some species grow offsets that can be removed.

Manfreda sileri

A narrow-leaved rosette of soft concave fleshy green leaves reaching 50 cm long, spotted with darker blotches and fine marginal teeth. A very long inflorescence up to 60 cm high produces whitish flowers that open from a tubular base to 6 petals and large anthers on the stamens.

Manfreda virginica

This species comes from West Virginia, Missouri and Florida, where it tolerates cold to –29°C. The soft leaves are 6–8 cm wide and up to 40 cm long, and are mottled brown to purple. The inflorescence reaches 1.8 m high and bears fragrant green to yellow flowers. Propagation is from seed or offsets.

Above: *Manfreda sileri.*

Above: *Ochagavia carnea.*

OCHAGAVIA

Bromeliaceae

The pink flowers of this plant from Chile always attract attention. It grows on arid mountain slopes in its natural habitat, but in temperate zones is useful in the drier areas as a groundcovering plant, soon clumping to spread over several metres given good soil.

Ochagavia carnea

Linear-toothed, light silver-green leaves up to 50 cm long form the rosettes of this clumping plant. The central inflorescence is made up of densely packed pink flowers, each about 5 cm long and surrounded by white woolly bracts.

Above: *Opthalmophyllum dinteri.*

OPTHALMOPHYLLUM

Aizoaceae

This genus, very similar to lithops, is from Namibia and Cape Province in South Africa where dry conditions prevail.

Their succulent bodies have shiny translucent tops to let the light into the plant; most species are green but some have a reddish colouring in the 2–3 cm long leaves and the flowers are usually white or pink.

Treat the same as lithops, with full sunlight and water only in warm weather. Free-draining potting mix is essential. The older leaves shrivel back to form a collar around the new ones. Propagation from seed.

Opthalmophyllum dinteri

This plant has a green body consisting of a pair of thick green leaves, slightly reddish on the sides with translucent smooth tops. The flowers arising between the leaves are pink.

OTHONNA

Aizoaceae

Some forms of Othonna, native to Africa, are caudiciforms with thickened bases and stems that can be grown in containers or rockeries, while others are trailing groundcovers.

Othonna capensis

A mat-forming prostrate-growing plant from South Africa. It has thick cylindrical green leaves 2 cm long. The small daisy-like yellow flowers grow on thin stems reaching 15 cm high. Propagates easily from pieces.

Above: *Othonna capensis*.

PACHYPHYTUM

Crassulaceae

Pachyphytums are Mexican succulents related to echeverias, so need the same general treatment. The very fat fleshy leaves attract attention and the flowers, often reddish, are very pretty. The bloom brushes off very easily in handling as do the leaves, so care is essential.

Pachyphytum amethysum

This plant has short thick cylindrical leaves, light greenish blue with pink tips and branching from the base. Propagation is from leaves that produce babies from the stem end.

Pachyphytum compactum

This plant branches tightly with very closely set leaves near the crowns; the green leaves are short thick and angular, wide at the base and pointed, with a patchy bloom on the surface. Propagate from cuttings.

Above: *Pachyphytum compactum*.

Pachyphytum kimnachi

These branching plants are up to 10 cm high, and have rosettes of semi-cyclindrical leaves about 3–4 cm long and 1 cm wide, changing colour during the year from a pale grey to a warm apricot shade, making it a useful plant for massed colour effect. Propagate from leaves or cuttings.

Pachyphytum oviferum

Sometimes called moonstones, this species has very thick oval leaves rather like the old-fashioned sugared almonds. They can be quite white with a heavy coating of bloom when grown indoors, but in very sheltered dry outdoor areas, the sun brings out a pinkish colour in the leaves. The beautiful flowers hang down, white sepals almost hiding the reddish petals beneath. Propagate from leaves or stem with a crown.

Top left: *Pachyphytum kimnachi*; top right and above: *P. oviferum*.

PACHYPODIUM

Apocynaceae

Water-storing plants from South Africa and Madagascar, pachypodium occupy dry habitats and survive by means of their caudex. They are best propagated from seed or by grafting.

Pachypodium lamerei

This species is one of the most commonly grown pachypodiums, but doesn't like cold conditions. It has a single unbranched trunk, wider one quarter of the way up than elsewhere, and covered in spirally arranged tubercles with 3 stiff sharp spines pointing outwards from each one. Given ideal conditions, it can reach 1.5 m from seed in 5 years, after which it should flower; in the wild it can reach 8 m in height and 60 cm in diameter, the bottle-shaped trunk forking into thick erect branches. The dark green linear leaves can grow up to 30 cm long and are contained in the top few centimetres of the stem, while scented white flowers 6–10 cm across are produced terminally.

Pachypodium lealii var. *saundersii*

Another plant with a very broad base and stems with three spines at intervals along each one. The green leaves grow to 8 cm, the flowers are white.

Pachypodium rosulatum

This species has a large caudex, forked prickly stems to 3 m, and yellow flowers with individual thin stems.

Top: *Pachypodium lealii* var. *saundersii*; above: *P. rosulatum* in flower.

Pachypodium succulentum

This plant also grows a caudex and has spiny stems rising from the base. Green leaves grow to 8 cm, the flowers are pink.

PACHYVERIA

Crassulaceae

Pachyveria are crosses between pachyphytums and echeverias, the two genera being very similar and hybridising freely.

Pachyveria pachyphytoides

This plant is of branching habit to about 15 cm and grows from a crown. It has thick oval to pointed light blue-grey leaves that age to reddish and yellow shades. Propagate with a piece of stem or from leaves.

Pachyveria 'Royal Flush'

The heavy rosette, to about 15 cm wide, is of dull reddish colouring and formed of thick semi-cylindrical upward pointing leaves. Propagation from leaves.

Top: *Pachyveria pachyphytoides*; above: *P. 'Royal Flush'*.

PLEISOPILUS

Aizoaceae

There are several species of these South African succulents with their very thick leaves; some have greyish leaves up to 9 cm long. They need dry conditions, so are well suited to growing with indoor collections. Water sparingly and only in summer. Propagation from seed.

Pleisopilus bolusii

These are solitary plants, with a pair of very thick grey-green keeled leaves with many fine raised dots of a darker green over them. The flowers are yellow and form between the two leaves in late summer.

Pleisopilus nelii

This is a handsome species with squat flat almost hemispherical leaves with a sharp-edged cleft. They are greyish green with dark green raised dots.

Above: *Pleisopilus bolusii.*

PORTULACA

Portulacaceae

There are many species of both annual and perennial portulaca endemic to warm dry regions of the world and all have soft fleshy leaves and stems that contain moisture to ensure they grow flowers and set seed before the drought arrives. Some of the perennials have tubers and in the dry regions of Australia and both North and South America there are many different species, most being prostrate herbs.

Portulaca grandiflora

Originally from Brazil, this is a useful summer annual. The low spreading plants have small cylindrical leaves about 1.5 cm long on red stems. The brightly coloured double flowers are 4–5 cm across in red, pink, yellow and white, with yellow stamens and all with notched petal ends; the flowers stand above a whorl of small leaves and tufts of hairs. Propagation from seed.

Portulaca oleracea

Also known as wild portulaca, this is a nuisance mat plant of sandy dry gardens, growing very quickly to 80–90 cm across in suitable conditions. It has red stems, flattened succulent green leaves with a narrow red margin, but in harsh conditions the leaves show much more red. The small 5–7.5 mm yellow flowers have notched petals. This is a nuisance weed so remove all plants before they set seeds.

Below: *Portulaca grandiflora*; bottom: *P. oleracea*.

PUYA

Bromeliaceae

Puyas come from high areas of Chile, Bolivia and Peru and grow well in subtropical and temperate areas. They produce rosettes of very spiny margined narrow leaves, and bell- or tubular-shaped flowers in unusual colours. Some will take many years to bloom. These plants require a free-draining very warm sunny spot. Propagation from seed or basal crowns.

Puya alpestris

This plant is multi-crowned and can spread to 2–3 m across when mature. It has narrow green leaves, silver on the reverse side, with outward-pointing spines. In late spring strong flower spikes reaching 2 m high suddenly appear, sending out short stiff spiky branches, the lower halves with buds that open to the most unusual metallic blue-green shade with bright orange anthers and much pollen. The flowers are tubular, about 5 cm long with three petals with a satiny appearance; gradually the buds towards the outer ends of the branches will bloom as the inner ones fade. Propagation from crowns cut off the root base.

Puya flavofirens

This species forms a cluster of rosettes of very thin narrow spiny leaves of silver green, almost a tangled appearance, but the pink flower stems and many pink bracts are most impressive. Dark green tubular flowers emerge from the pink stems making a great combination. Propagation from seed or basal crowns.

Top left and above: *Puya alpestris*.

Puya laxa

This has thick succulent speckled silver leaves.

Puya venusta

This appears to be a variable species, but the very silver forms are outstanding for foliage value and the well-spaced 50 cm rosettes are worthwhile in the spacious garden. As with other puyas, the foliage has spines. The branched inflorescence on one form of *P. venusta* arises on a pink stem to 120 cm and reddish bracts cover the purple three-petalled flowers and their yellow stamens. Propagation is from seed or crowns removed from the base of the plant.

Top right: *Puya flavofirens*; above and above left: *P. venusta*; left: *P. laxa*.

SEDUM

Crassulaceae

Although sedums are almost entirely endemic to the Northern Hemisphere, mainly central America and Asia, they have been taken to many areas of the world. Originally the northern ones were mainly coastal plants, but those originating from the tropical areas grew as alpines. Some sedums are very hardy, but others need protection if beyond the limit of their natural zone.

Sedums are commonly called stonecrops, a name that is also used for many other succulents when the true name isn't known. There are over 800 sedums in cultivation, some evergreen and others deciduous, and leaf forms and colourings cover an extensive range.

Sedums and allied plants from the sub-family Sedoideae (aeoniums, cotyledons, echeverias and sempervivums) have a special method of transpiration that enables them to avoid moisture loss in extreme conditions. Where most plants breath through open stomata (pores) during the daytime, these plants have reduced numbers of stomata on their leaves which open to breathe only at night. In order to do this the night-time temperature needs to be cooler than during the day, so if there is not a marked difference the stomata don't open at night and these plants can suffocate. In the scientific world, they are called CAM plants (Crassulacean Acidic Metabolism), and their ability to avoid water

Above: *Sedum* x *rubrotinctum*.

loss during the heat of the day is very important when they live in very hot, windy or arid conditions. Historical medicinal uses have been noted for one of the most common species, *Sedum acre*, which is said to have been used on wounds, as an emetic, an abortifacient, as a fomentation, a purgative and for gout, scurvy and haemorrhoids. *S. anglicum* was used to stop bleeding when taken internally, and externally for fevers, cankers and sores, and *S. reflexum* was recommended for heartburn and also used as a salad crop. In the garden sedums have many uses, often creating a background for larger-leaved succulents when planted as a groundcover. They are decorative in creative paving and good fillers in tubs, pots, window boxes, hanging baskets, on walls, in myriad containers and for neat edgings and lines in decorations such as planted clocks. The larger-leaved and usually bigger growing deciduous sedums flower in late summer and are very useful and colourful in herbaceous borders. Most sedums prefer to grow in light well-drained soil where a little general fertiliser will promote sturdy growth, but don't overdo it or uncharacteristic floppy growth will follow.

Propagation is usually easy from pieces or leaves and the deciduous varieties can be divided from the base.

EVERGREEN SPECIES

Sedum acre
One of the very small groundcovering sedums with green foliage, sometimes with a twist in the leaf arrangement, and masses of yellow flowers when in bloom.

Sedum adolphi
This species grows quite heavy compact heads of yellow-green foliage with smallish pointed leaves which are not as large or spread as far apart as in the similar yellow *S. nussbaumerianum*.

Sedum aytacianum
A small compact mounding plant from Turkey, it has very tiny green leaves, reddish stems and starry white flowers.

Top left: *Sedum acre*; above: *S. aytacianum*.

Opposite, top left: *Sedum burrito*; top right: *S. commixtum*; bottom: *S. decumbens*.

Sedum burrito

Commonly known as baby burro's tail, this plant has thick, almost oval, tightly packed light grey-green leaves, their weight causing the stems to hang over their container. It has wine-red flowers in spring.

Sedum commixtum

This is a hardy and commonly grown species from high Mexican mountains, and also one of the better blue-coloured succulents. The thick blue leaves in stemmed rosettes turn purple on the tips adding to the colourful effect, and every leaf that falls will grow. Side stems rise up from below the original crowns to about 35 cm high, creating a rather tangly appearance, but these can be easily removed. S. commixtum doesn't flower often, but when it does, small flowers are formed in spring in a loose cluster with yellow-green mottled brown petals. This species will withstand temperatures of -12°C if kept dry.

Sedum decumbens

This plant grows to about 30 cm, and is colourful in the garden with small rosettes of succulent bright yellow-green foliage. It bears yellow flowers in flattened clusters in spring, and is ideal as a dense groundcover.

Sedum lydium

This species forms a very low carpet of tiny stems, about 4 cm high, covered in green leaves that often turn bronze red. Tiny clusters of pink-white flowers grow on thin stems well above the foliage clusters. It likes to grow among rocks and paving for a cool root run and often dries out too much in containers.

Sedum mexicanum

Despite its name, it is interesting to note that this species didn't originate in Mexico; in fact it is thought to have come from Asia, but it has naturalised in many areas of the world and somehow acquired the name *mexicanum* – probably because a lot of sedums come from there. The plant forms spreading clumps about 25 cm high, and its foliage is light green but turns bright yellow at times, with numerous pointed cylindrical leaves pointing upwards. It has yellow flowers, and appears to need more moisture in summer than most succulents.

Sedum morganianum

Commonly called burro's tail, this is definitely a plant for hanging baskets with its heavily laden stems that hang down. Thick, tapering blue-green leaves are crowded on the stems, and the flowers are pink.

Top left: *Sedum spathulifolium* and *S. lydium* (smaller plant); above: *S. morganianum*; left: *S. mexicanum.*

Sedum nussbaumerianum
(formerly known as S. adolphi
in New Zealand)

This is a branching plant reaching about 45 cm, with rosettes of gold to bronze leaves which are larger, flatter, wider and not as pointed as the true *S. adolphi*, but which adds exciting colour to the garden, containers or collection. Flowers are white. Plants can get leggy eventually, needing breaking up and pieces rooted to start again.

Sedum pachyphyllum

This is a very useful garden plant when massed. The thick light blue-grey leaves have red tips and yellow flowers appear in spring. It stands dryness and tolerates a fair amount of wet and cold, and a group planting will last several years before rejuvenation is needed. Rejuvenation is easy: simply break off crowns with about 6 cm of stem, allow to dry and replant.

Sedum palmeri

This plant has rosettes of thin flattish leaves of light glaucous blue-green on stems that arch a little and are up to 30 cm long. The flowers are yellow. As a dense mound of foliage the plant is useful, being hardy and tolerating much cold if kept dry.

Top: *Sedum nussbaumerianum*; middle: *S. pachyphyllum*; right: *S. palmeri*.

Sedum x rubrotinctum

This is the very popular jelly bean plant. It is thought to be a hybrid of S. *pachyphyllum* and S. *stahlii* and is well known for its leaves which turn red at times. The leaves are arranged in a unique spiral around the stems, and the flowers are yellow. This sedum tolerates winters in mild areas, needs little care and every leaf that falls will grow a new plant.

Sedum spathulifolium

There are a number of forms of this sedum in cultivation, which has attractive ground-hugging rosettes, often covered in a heavy white bloom, although red shows up at times. Flowers are yellow.

Sedum spurium

There are many forms of this flat-leaved plant that creeps about with branched stems. The serrated foliage turns to bronze and purple shades at times, and the flowers are pink. It looks well among rocks.

Sedum stahlii

Thin prostrate stems, small crowded almost oval and slightly hairy reddish green leaves and yellow flowers are features of this plant.

Sedum treleasei

This plant has thick light blue-green leaves in terminal rosettes, but the leaves persist on the stems which can lengthen to about 30 cm; branches form from the base only. It is fairly cold hardy if kept dry.

Top left: *Sedum stahlii*; bottom left: S. *treleasei*; below: S. *spurium*.

DECIDUOUS SPECIES

Sedum alboroseum 'Frosty Morn'

Originally from Japan, this plant journeyed to the United States, then to England and New Zealand and has upright growth to about 60 cm. It has green leaves edged with white, and attractive flowers, white with a pink centre.

Sedum alboroseum 'Mediovariegatum'

This is a handsome plant growing to about 60 cm. The soft glaucous green of the species is carried on the margins of the leaves with a robust creamy yellow coming through the stems and the greater area of the leaves. The flowers have white petals and rosy carpels which create a pinkish effect. When the plant resorts to occasional plain green growths they should be removed at the base.

Top left: *Sedum alboroseum* 'Mediovariegatum'; top right and above: *S. alboroseum* 'Frosty Morn'.

Sedum 'Bertram Anderson'

A low-growing plant with bluish grey to purple leaves, and deep pink flowers.

Sedum Herbstfreude

Commonly known as 'Autumn Joy', this cultivar is not new but still an excellent strong-growing reliable plant reaching about 60 cm. It has clusters of deep pink flowers in late summer, these holding on as tan-coloured heads into the winter.

Sedum hidakanum
(syn. Hylotelephium pluricaule)

A low-spreading plant, thought to be a hybrid, with splendid blue to purple leaves, and attractive pink flowers. It appears to be very suitable for container growing or among rocks in the garden.

Sedum 'Purple Emperor'

This upright-growing plant reaches about 45 cm high, and has attractive longish and heavily serrated deep purple leaves. Ruby pinkish flowers appear in late summer.

Sedum sieboldii

This is a glaucous blue-leaved species with a spreading habit ideal for container growing. Deep pink margins with shallow scallops add interest to the leaves, which are attached to the stem in unusual trios. Flowers are pink, blooming in autumn after which the plant defoliates and remains dormant until the next spring.

This page, top: *Sedum hidakanum*; right: S. 'Bertram Anderson'.

Opposite, top: *Sedum sieboldii*; bottom: S. 'Purple Emperor'.

Sedum sieboldii 'Mediovariegatum'

This has similar growth habit to *S. sieboldii*, but the variegated foliage adds interest and it tends to colour much more than the straight species. There are several different clones of this form.

Sedum spectabile 'Stardust'

A strong green-leaved plant in tidy clumps which reaches about 60 cm high. It has spectacular flat-topped clusters of small white flowers. This plant makes a good display for some weeks while still in bud, and the flowers stay pure white with no hint of pink appearing.

Sedum telephium 'Matrona'

A strong upright plant about 90 cm high, with long-ish oval purplish green leaves with light serrations, and large heads of most attractive pale pink flowers.

Sedum telephium 'Morchen'

The dark almost chocolate-brown foliage on this plant reaches about 70 cm high, and above this are rounded heads of deep pink flowers, which age to a deep mahogany brown.

Sedum telephium 'Munstead Red'

This compact-growing cultivar reaching 60 cm bears very deep red flowers that last well in clusters above green-tinged red foliage. The flowers age well to an attractive reddish brown.

Sedum 'Vera Jamieson'

A low-spreading plant with glaucous blue-grey leaves, and deep pink flowers.

Top: *Sedum* 'Vera Jamieson'; left: *S. telephium* 'Munstead Red'.

Top and above: *Sedum spectabile* 'Stardust'.

Top and above: *Sedum telephium* 'Matrona'.

SEMPERVIVUM

Crassulaceae

The name sempervivum stems from the custom of planting the ridges of thatched roofs with these succulents to protect the houses from lightning (semper means forever or always and vivum means alive). Whether the safeguard worked we will never know, but another name relating to their use on buildings is houseleek, while a third common name, hen and chickens, refers to the method of reproduction.

The sempervivums, native to southern and central Europe, are frost-hardy and grow happily in temperate climates; there is also one species from Morocco but it is susceptible to frosts.

Sempervivums are neat and tidy rosettes, ideal for small gardens where a group of different species or cultivars can be very attractive. Leaves vary in colouring from green through greys, browns, reds and maroons, sometimes with coloured leaf tips and sometimes with colour at the base of the leaves. Sempervivums show marked seasonal changes in their leaf colour: with winter showing the dullest

colours while from spring through summer the colours intensify. There are many named hybrids apart from the true species and many of the modern hybrids will grow into bigger rosettes than the original species. The flowers on sempervivums are open, starry and usually pink and held above the plant on a stem bearing several flowers. Unfortunately the crown that produces the flowerhead is monocarpic, and always dies off after flowering, but there are usually 'chickens' produced previously from the base and that grow in a ring around the mother plant, some still attached by a thin stem. This umbilical cord can be severed and the new plants will grow on from their own roots, but sometimes the mother plant does not reproduce and the variety can be lost entirely.

An extract from S. *tectorum*, one of the European species, has been used to treat burns.

Sempervivums will grow well in full sun in temperate climates, but will also do well with a little shade for part of the day. In very hot dry weather they tend to shrink down and lose colouring but most recover after rain or watering. They are frost hardy in areas where most other succulents would suffer.

Interesting combinations of these rosettes in bowls or tubs with fine gravel as a mulch will keep tidy for a long time, and look good in courtyards or window boxes. Although a few old leaves need removing annually from the base of the rosettes, the plants don't shed them freely so no leaf litter is spread

This page: *Sempervivum* cultivars.

Opposite: *Sempervivum* 'Director Jacobs'.

Sempervivum arachnoideum

Commonly known as the 'cobwebs plant', the specific name coming from the word 'arachnid', which refers to spiders, this species from southern Europe is always a favourite and a charming plant for children to grow. Neat green leaves, lots of babies and the fascinating 'spiderwebs' are features that stand out in a group of sempervivums. The flowers, held in a cluster on a stem above the rosette, are deep pink in colour.

Sempervivum 'Butterbur'

This plant has rosettes reaching about 16 cm, and has an attractive formal shape and colouring. The central colour often contrasts with the outer leaves of olive green.

Sempervivum calcareaum

A blue-green European species, 4-6 cm wide, with red-tipped leaves and pink flowers.

This page, left: *Sempervivum arachnoideum*; below: S. 'Amtmann Fischer'.

Opposite, top left: *Sempervivum* 'Butterbur'; top right: S. 'Crimsonette'; middle: S. 'Eminent'; bottom: S. 'Grammens'.

about, making them ideal for those who prefer maintenance-free paths.

Propagation is usually from offsets, otherwise they can be grown from seed; because they hybridise freely, seedlings may not always be true to the parent.

Sempervivum 'Amtmann Fischer'

One of the largest varieties of sempervivum, reaching 20–30 cm wide, it goes through seasonal colour changes of grey green to reddish and lavender.

Sempervivum **'Crimsonette'**

Grows between 8–15 cm wide, and has green outer leaves and bright crimson centres, although in some seasons all leaves turn red. Produces many offsets.

Sempervivum **'Director Jacobs'**

Not a big plant, but one with numerous tightly packed leaves, reddish with light green contrasting new leaves in early summer.

Sempervivum **'Eminent'**

Narrowish leaves of deep red fading to olive green make this an outstanding cultivar reaching 10–18 cm wide.

Sempervivum **'Fluffy Fluke'**

This plant has larger rosettes than S. *arachnoideum*, but the many fine hairs on the green leaf margins of this plant tend to look like webs at first glance.

Sempervivum **'Grammens'**

This is a hybrid, bred from S. *tectorum atropurpureum* x S. *atroviolaceum*. It is a large grower with upright leaves in a big rosette around 20–25 cm, with interesting colours ranging from deep maroon to soft lavender.

Sempervivum 'Grey Lady'

This plant produces flattish rounded rosettes 8–17 cm wide in a tight neat formation. Leaves are greyish green to maroon and change with the seasons.

Sempervivum 'Kappa'

A strongly clumping form with rosettes 8–10 cm wide, in colours of olive green to dull red.

Sempervivum 'Lavender and Old Lace'

The soft lavender colouring and finely-toothed leaf edges create a lacy effect which has given rise to the name of this cultivar.

Sempervivum 'Maytime'

This plant has a very neat rosette 6–8 cm wide, of dark brownish red leaves edged with contrasting bright green leaves.

Sempervivum 'More Honey'

A greenish leaved variety which changes to orange red at times. It sends out chicks abundantly.

Sempervivum 'Oddity'

This plant gets its name from the unusual rolled green leaves with dark red tips that curve back to make what appears to be a tubular leaf.

Sempervivum potsii

Quite a small sempervivum, growing to about 3 cm, but the bright light green of the rosettes adds contrasting colour within a group of mixed cultivars or species. It sends out babies freely.

Top left: *Sempervivum* 'Kappa'; above: S. 'Oddity'; left: S. 'Maytime'.

Sempervivum 'Red Devil'

This variety reaching 8–15 cm clumps well, and has upward pointing leaves with distinctive red colouring.

Sempervivum 'Royanum'

A cultivar of S. *tectorum*, this plant has good-sized firm tight rosettes reaching 8–15 cm. It is green with red tips, and the shade of green changes with the seasons from very deep rich green to yellow green. There are very seldom any offsets.

Sempervivum 'Sir William Lawrence'

This is a cultivar of S. *calcareum*, and is very similar, reaching 8–10 cm in diameter. It produces leaves of a deep blue-green shade with deep maroon tips.

Sempervivum 'Spangle'

Has similar webbing to S. *arachnoideum* but a much bigger rosette, 6–9 cm. It also shows red colouring under the leaves at times.

Sempervivum tectorum

This species from southern European mountain areas is sometimes confused with S. *calcareum*. It has glaucous grey-green leaves with broad red tips, although the shade of green and the amount of red marking can vary. Clusters of starry flowers on tall stalks are light red in colour.

Sempervivum 'Unicorn'

Green to rosy pink leaves with reddish tips are among the seasonal changes of colouring on this large plant. Many chicks are produced on long stolons.

Top: *Sempervivum* 'Sir William Lawrence'; right: S. 'Spangle'.

SENECIO

Asteraceae

Some of the succulent senecios come from the Northern Hemisphere: from Mexico, the Canary Islands and the Middle East, but a large number also grow in South Africa. Many of the 100 plus species grow to be large bushes, but several of the blue-foliaged plants are used as groundcovers. Propagation from cuttings.

Senecio grantii

This species is of open growth, has broad leaves and daisy-like red flowers on long thin stems.

Seneci haworthii

A species growing to about 30 cm, with narrow cylindrical leaves heavily coated with a white meal. Flowers are orange-yellow. It prefers to be kept dry and cannot handle outdoor conditions in some areas.

Senecio mandraliscae

This is the larger of the two glaucous blue forms commonly grown as groundcovers, and can reach about 45 cm, although it is advisable to prune out the centre to keep it lower and bushier. The cylindrical pointed leaves are about 6 cm long, and the dull white flowers uninteresting.

Senecio serpens

Reaching 15 cm in height, S. serpens has cylindrical glaucous blue leaves, grooved above and blunt tipped, and in hot dry conditions the leaf tips sometimes change colour to a purplish shade. Tight heads of small cream flowers are held above the foliage.

Top left: Senecio mandraliscae with S. serpens in foreground; top right: S. serpens; above: S. grantii.

STAPELIA

Asclepiadaceae

Stapelias are strange little plants from South-west Africa and South Africa and a few from tropical areas in the East Indies. In the Karroo Desert, South Africa, they get summer rain and flower soon after.

The common feature of stapelias is the unpleasant odour of the flowers. One species, *Stapelia gigantea* has flowers which can reach between 10–40 cm in diameter, but the species more commonly grown have smaller flowers.

Grown indoors they need good drainage, the flowers forming on the base of the stems of current growth.

Stapelias can be propagated by division or seed.

Above: *Stapelia asterias lucida*; right: *S. hirsuta.*

Stapelia asterias lucida

This species has 4-angled stems, and really thickened leaves reaching 10–20 cm tall, with small spines down the ridges. A huge bud for the size of the plant opens out to a wide star-shaped flower 10–15 cm across, with hairy reddish petals and emitting a disgusting odour which attracts pollinating insects.

Stapelia hirsuta

This stapelia has leaves that are green thickened stems with small hairy tufts and spines on the edges of the 4 angles. It has very hairy 10–12 cm flowers with an extra fringe of hairs on the petal margins, and transverse bands of light yellow on brownish red petals. As with other stapelias, the flowers exude an odour to attract insect pollinators and sometimes blowflies lay their eggs on the flower believing that it is rotting meat.

SYNADENIUM

Euphorbiaceae

There are about 20 species in this genus of succulent shrubs or small trees which come from tropical America, tropical Africa and Madagascar. All have a milky white latex-like sap that is poisonous and can be a skin and eye irritant for many people.

They prefer sunny to partially shaded sites, are drought tolerant and are happy in well-drained average soil. Propagation usually from cuttings, but sometimes from seed.

Synadenium grantii

This shrub, reaching about 3 m high with rubbery wine-coloured stems, is native to tropical east Africa. It has fleshy, almost diamond-shaped greyish green leaves 14–20 cm long, with prominent midribs and lateral veining. Panicles of small red flowers appear year round.

Synadenium grantii 'Rubra'

Also known as 'northern dead man's tree', this is an ornamental shrub from Uganda, Tanzania and Mozambique. The plant has thick branches and fleshy oval leaves 10–15 cm long, wine red in colour with a purple underside, or sometimes spotted with red on deep green. The sap of the tree is milky white and very poisonous. Cuttings of this tree grow amazingly fast in warm sheltered conditions.

Above: *Synadenium grantii* 'Rubra' (spotted form); left: *S. grantii* 'Rubra' (dark red form).

YUCCA

Agavaceae

Yuccas come from the southern United States, Mexico and Guatemala and some of the Caribbean islands, and are generally very hardy plants, although a few of them from warmer areas cannot be expected to withstand heavy frosts. Yuccas from the Caribbean are well suited to temperate coastal areas and are very useful for landscaping in the driest sandy spots.

The popular *Yucca aloifolia* is known to have been in cultivation from about 1600 and since then has been taken all round the world as an ornamental plant. Yuccas have been used for many purposes by the indigenous peoples of their native habitats: the leaves for basket making and even the roots of *Y. brevifolia* worked into the basket for a red-coloured accent. Leaves were also used as a thatch over yucca trunks for shelter, and pounded until fibres were left to make small paintbrushes for decorating pottery. Spanish and English explorers and settlers used yucca fibre in ropes, chair seats and to hang meat.

Wood from trunks of Joshua trees (*Y. brevifolia)* was used to make medical splints — it was light, pliable and strong, gave good air circulation. At one stage in the 1890s a factory in Los Angeles was set up to make these splints. High-quality paper could also be made from Joshua trees, but over-use resulted in the establishment of the Joshua Tree National Park to limit their felling.

Y. elephantipes flowers are said to be good fried with eggs. Some European settlers cooked the flowers like cabbage; since then these have even been canned and sold commercially. Yucca flowering stalks are roasted, peeled and eaten like sugar cane, while the roots of *Y. elata* (the soaptree yucca) and *Y. glauca* (soapweed) were pounded either fresh or dried for a soapy lather.

Y. elata and *Y. glauca* leaves were chopped and ground with cotton meal for cattle food early in the 20th century — machines were even invented to help

Above: *Yucca aloifolia.*

grind up the leaves and had names like 'The Ideal Yucca Chopper' and 'Krack Jack S.S. Cutter'.

All yuccas need free-draining soil, and are best planted with the crown of the plant slightly raised above ground level so that when the soil sinks a little the crown doesn't end up in a hollow that will gather moisture and rot the plant.

Yucca aloifolia

Commonly called the 'Spanish Dagger', this yucca has a natural distribution over a wide area of southern United States, some of the Caribbean islands, Mexico and Guatemala. It is commonly found on sand dunes and is believed to have been cultivated since about 1600 with the first flowering in England recorded in 1604. The slightly curved 60 cm long green leaves spiral round the base or stem which can reach up to 3 m with occasional branches. Sharp spines adorn the leaf terminals and the waxy white flowers are dramatic in dense panicles about 2 m long. Because this plant is hardy and easily propagated from seed, offsets and stem or root cuttings, it is a popular plant in many countries.

Yucca aloifolia tricolor

A central band of bold yellow stands out against the green leaf margins in this form.

Yucca aloifolia var.

This variegated form has attractive yellow-edged leaves, and sometimes the flowers have a hint of mauve in them.

Yucca brevifolia

The Joshua tree is a very large grower of dramatic form, with an average height of 9–15 m, although it has been recorded at 24 m. It is the outstanding tree in the Mojave Desert, parts of Nevada and Arizona and is much used ornamentally elsewhere. The tree branches sometimes bend to right angles and the old leaves usually cling to these, except on very old specimens when they drop off, exposing interesting patterns on dark brown branches. The grey to blue-green leaves are rigid, 15–30 cm long and sharply pointed with minute marginal teeth. The inflorescence, up to 50 cm long, bends over with the weight of its 6 cm long, cream to white closed flowers, which have an unpleasant odour. It is said to tolerate cold to -18°C.

Yucca elephantipes

Grown widely for its dramatic upright form, this yucca comes from the warm areas of the Mexican coast to Guatemala. Plants can reach 9 m in height, usually with many basal stems forming. The spineless green leaves radiate from the top of the stem, but often hang down as they age, and the short panicle of small bell-shaped cream to white flowers appears from within the crown of leaves. It has been transported to many Mediterranean-type climates around the world, but has been known to survive -3°C. This very versatile plant is tolerant of a range of light conditions from full sun to shade, and will even grow successfully indoors. Stem cuttings of any size can be used for propagation.

Yucca elephantipes 'Siesta'

This cultivar is an attractive form of Y. elephantipes, with yellow variegation on the margins providing colour for landscaping use.

Yucca elephantipes 'Silver Star'

Another cultivar of Y. elephantipes, this has striking foliage, excellent for tub use or for planting out.

Yucca flaccida

This species from eastern United States is a very hardy plant with bunching rosettes of deep green to glaucous green leaves that recurve, hence the name 'flaccida'. Inflorescences about 2 m long are held above the leaves, with pendent cream to white flowers. This plant will tolerate more cold and wet than other yuccas, in fact winter temperatures down to -29°C do not worry it, but it will still perform well in sun or partial shade. Propagation by offsets or seed.

Yucca 'Garland's Gold'

A New Zealand-raised cultivar with soft leaves about 70 cm long, with a central gold band edged with green. The young leaves are upright in the centre of each stemless plant and as they mature the older ones reflex from half their length creating a graceful effect. An excellent garden plant: not too big and not prickly!

This page: *Yucca* 'Garland's Gold'.

Opposite: *Yucca elephantipes*.

Above: *Yucca rigida.*

Yucca gloriosa

This is a multiple-stemmed shrub growing 2–4 m tall, from coastal areas of eastern United States. It sometimes branches near the tops where rosettes of straight spineless glaucous green leaves grow to about 40 cm long; the older leaves tend to be self grooming, leaving the bare trunks visible. An

inflorescence arises within the head of leaves on a 1 m long stalk, and white flowers tinged with purple or red usually appear late summer to autumn. This yucca grows best in warm conditions, full sun and good drainage, although leaves can burn in extremely sunny conditions. It will tolerate partial shade so is quite versatile, but won't stand cold below -6°C. Propagation from stem cuttings, offsets or seed.

Yucca rigida

Commonly known as the blue yucca, this species can ultimately reach 3–4.5 m in height, and is usually single trunked but is known to branch after flowering. In its early years it has a perfect sphere of narrow spine-tipped light blue-grey leaves about 70 cm long; older dead leaves remain attached to the trunk on mature plants. The creamy white flowers are in a panicle growing to 1 m. This yucca likes full sun but can be grown in partial shade, and is drought tolerant, withstanding cold to -12°C. It needs good drainage and is an excellent plant for landscaping with such wonderful colour. Propagation from seed.

Yucca whipplei

This species grows naturally in southern and Baja California, and has many stiff thin sharply-pointed greyish green to bluish grey leaves in a stemless dense rosette. The inflorescence can be up to 4 m tall, and has many small branches with hundreds of white, sometimes purple-tipped flowers, but the plant dies after flowering. *Y. whipplei* is a very hardy plant for either sunny or cold areas, and tolerates richer soils better than some species. Propagation from seed or offsets.

INDEX

Page numbers in **bold** refer to illustrations.